AIR21
Delta's Debacle

Legal Lessons Learned and Shared
to Save Your Career and Improve Safety

Aviation. Inspiration. Motivation.

at

www.KarlenePetitt.com

DEDICATION

To LEE SEHAM, thank you for teaching me the law and for your everlasting friendship.

Air21
Delta's Debacle

Legal Lessons Learned and Shared
to Save Your Career and Improve Safety

Karlene K. Petitt

JET STAR PUBLISHING INC.
SEATAC WA

Contents

Introduction

WINNING IS NOT always about right or wrong, it's about meeting legal standards where corporate power and money to sustain the fight often dictate the verdict. Those in the wrong will fight with creativity and distortions of the truth, and corporate attorneys will say anything on behalf of their clients. Those you sue can sustain the financial drain because they have insurance to cover their legal fees, while you pay out of pocket. However, this legal fight is not hopeless as I have proven in *Petitt vs. Delta*.[1]

Knowledge of the law and your legal rights are essential to win. If someone is gunning for you, you must take steps to protect yourself. Similar to creating a flight plan and pre-flighting your aircraft prior to departure, you must take the steps to ensure success.

Have you experienced retaliation? Are you anticipating retaliation? Are you contemplating reporting a safety concern but fear retaliation? Are you wondering if you have a case? I'm certain this book will answer all those questions and more. Most importantly, this will increase your chances of succeeding on the legal playing field by being prepared.

This is a playbook of the AIR21 statute and how and why I beat Delta Air Lines. More so, this is a lesson plan to ensure your success in safely reporting your concerns, with knowledge that the law will protect you.

Delta placed passenger safety in harm's way—their first mistake. The second was to gaslight the wrong woman. The third was they went to court with a losing case. This event was Delta's debacle, but the experience taught me many things, which I will share with you throughout these pages.

Your job is to prepare yourself for the legal battle. That preparation begins with understanding Federal and State laws. This book will explain the AIR21 statute and how to protect yourself before you report your concerns. Also, if you think your management team is gunning for you, there are strategies to oppose that attack within these pages by using this law. There is also a section on how to get those bastards who have lied and defamed you, and another on saving your sanity in the process with thoughts on how to move forward after this challenge ends. Challenge is nothing but a polite word for the hell you will experience.

You can safely report safety. You can stand up to retaliation. You can win your case. But not necessarily because you're right and they are wrong. You must meet all elements of the statute and be knowledgeable about the process. As the captain of your life, you know your story better than anyone, therefore your involvement is essential.

Your attorney knows the law (or should). You know your regulations, work rules, company policies, and the events better than any attorney or judge. Your fight must be a collaboration. There is also a great deal of work to do before you meet an attorney. If you're organized, efficient, and concise you will not only help the attorney to determine if you have a case but will keep your expenses inline during the process when you do.

When you file a lawsuit against another entity, be it an individual or corporation, don't think they will fold to avoid spending money to fight you. Quite the opposite. The Respondent is not paying attorney fees out of their pocket. Be it a corporation, a savvy businessman, or a neighbor, these entities and people have an umbrella policy—a clause in an insurance policy that covers their legal fees if sued. You, however, must pay your own legal fees because you are taking action against someone else.

What about a contingency fee relationship?

Today, contingency is virtually impossible with an AIR21 claim, the Aviation Whistleblower Law. I will explain why, later. Therefore, you'll be the financer, and will want to make the process as efficient as possible. I battled Delta Air Lines for seven years. I endured and succeeded, as you can as well. However, there are specific reasons that I prevailed, and I will share those with you, so you can do the same. I will also provide you the airline industry's strategy playbook and how you can fight it.

A little history on my case first. I provided a safety report to senior Delta Air Lines management. Naïve, I thought that these executives in the ivory tower were unaware of what was ongoing beyond their glass walls. I was wrong. There was no glass wall but an iron curtain. The unsafe operations were nothing but management playing a game of Russian Roulette with passengers' lives—a for-profit business decision. Shortly after I identified and internally reported numerous safety concerns Delta management removed me from duty.

In 2015 a vice president at Delta Air Lines, Captain James Graham, plotted to send me to a psychiatric evaluation simply because I requested a meeting with him to report safety concerns. In 2016 the airline's in-house attorney, Chris Puckett, employed a hitman dressed as a doctor to destroy my credibility and strip me of flying privileges. Delta paid Dr. David B. Altman $74,000, who then issued a fabricated mental health diagnosis disqualifying me from flight.

After an extensive Soviet Union style interrogation called a medical evaluation, this doctor diagnosed me as bipolar. Delta's intent was not simply to remove me from their airline, but to eradicate me from the industry as evidenced by the doctor they employed and the company's collaboration with him. Perhaps the goal was to discredit my doctoral research that corroborated Delta's unsafe operating practices or set an example for any other pilot who might come forward. Regardless as to why, our battle began. I filed a complaint under the OSHA Whistleblower Protection Act, the AIR21 statute, and the rest is history.

You cannot always trust people, and life is not fair. More so, there is no room for fairness in the courtroom, only the law. I am familiar with several cases of which I know the employee was correct in their assertions that airline management retaliated, but the case did not fit the AIR21 statute, or the employee missed their statute of limitations, and they lost.

This book will tell you if your case has merit for an AIR21 complaint, and how to ensure you will have a case that will stand up in court as well as explain the process. But also, how to protect yourself if you anticipate the company has you in their crosshairs, or if you plan to report a violation of a safety regulation. In my case, the universe had prepared me for this battle and provided guidance that I listened to throughout. I struggled the first year and that, too, I will explain, because the challenge with knowing the difference between good advice and bad can be daunting.

It's important to listen to advice of those with experience and be cognizant when support arrives, but also when not to trust those who are assisting your demise. This is only possible if you have knowledge and understand what tools you'll need to achieve success.

Never sit on your ass and do nothing. Do not pull the blanket over your head. Pilots continue flying the plane to the ground, despite the catastrophe. You do not have to be a pilot to adopt this philosophy in life. Do not give up and become a victim in your life. You are the protagonist and can direct this chapter no matter how dark it feels.

Despite years of safety experience, extensive education, and a logical brain, I had placed my faith in an attorney who advertised he knew the Whistleblower law. He did not. However, all the other attorneys I had contacted prior to him told me I did not have a case until after termination. They, too, were wrong. It took me a year to learn that my first attorney had never experienced an AIR21 case prior to mine. When I learned of this and challenged the fact, he asserted that any case in front of an Administrative Law Judge (ALJ) was the same thing. That, too, was incorrect.

A year into this battle and many thousands of dollars invested, a Seattle law firm heard of my case from a fellow pilot and wanted to take it on contingency; but only if I dropped my safety claims and proceeded with an action based on gender discrimination. Granted, a woman bringing safety concerns to Delta was the worst kind of offense in management's eyes, especially when she held more education, more type ratings, and more flight training experience than either of the two executive pilots she met with. To make matters worse, even my pilot union, ALPA, worked with the company against me. Not because I was wrong, but because ALPA leaders at Delta traditionally flow into management if they play ball. What Delta wanted, ALPA gave them. Delta wanted me gone.

My case was about safety, but this new law firm wanted to fight it on contingency if I chose gender over safety. I suspect gender was, in part, Captain Graham's source of consternation, but safety was the issue that needed fighting. Man or woman, it does not matter, we would all die on the plane in the same manner if we permit the erosion of safety standards. I felt lost. I prayed for an answer as what to do and which way to turn. Then the phone rang.

My ERAU law professor, an attorney, Captain John Sable, called to see how I was doing. Floundering was the most accurate answer to that question. I told him I had no faith in the knowledge of my highly paid attorney, ALPA was working against me, and some law firm would take my case on contingency but only if I dropped my safety concerns. He asked if I had spoken to Attorney Lee Seham. I had not. I called Lee, and the next level of education ensued. I paid him for an hour conference call to ask a few questions, and he explained the law. I fired my original attorney, employed Lee, and my world changed overnight for the better.

Lee knew the law and invited me to become involved in my case. I highly suggest you do the same—become involved in your case. Learn the law.

I turned down the contingency and battled on with my safety claims, despite the heavy financial burden. Yes, I could have filed both safety and gender. However, I knew I would return and did not want Delta and ALPA to turn my battle into a "girl" thing. Ironically, that is exactly what Delta claimed in their defense.

I am grateful to my first attorney for filing my case because the AIR21 statute has only a 90-day statute of limitation, the shortest of any law. The journey to trial swallowed four years of my life and lasted nine days over several months, with years of legal battles to follow. There was no jury of my peers, but instead a Federal Judge. This Administrative Law Judge, ALJ, would decide my fate. I faced off against the most powerful airline in the world. At that time, and perhaps today, Delta held more power and influence than any other carrier worldwide. But I now had Lee Seham on my side, and he was prepared with knowledge, integrity, and writing skills.

Management used their self-proclaimed dominance to get what they wanted, and they wanted me gone. Delta controlled not only the pilot union, but the FAA and far too many lobbyists. They paid a doctor for a false medical examination, bought off an arbitrator to win a grievance, and owned the pilot union, ALPA. When caught in their dirty deeds there was no accountability, despite senior airline management violating federal regulations, violating their own policies, and placing passenger lives in harm's way. Lack of accountability has proven a grave flaw in the safety system.

My fight began about the safety of our traveling public, it turned into a war of demanding justice. My battle was one of right versus wrong, not subjective opinions. My case met the law. This book will ensure yours does too.

People will die on an aircraft because of those who look the other way for money and power, or fear of job loss. People will die in hospitals because people fear the same. Complacency, looking the other way, and fear thrive. That we must change. The examples of death by airplane or misdiagnosis spread throughout history. Yet few seem to care, or perhaps they did not know how to fight the good fight. I cared. If you are reading this book, you do as well. And I will teach you how to have the best chance of winning your legal case.

In the end, Delta engaged in a war of attrition against me, of what ultimately became a war of wills. I wish I had known what I'm about to tell you before I began. But I was fortunate in having met the master of AIR21 litigation, Lee Seham. His son, Sam Seham, is now following in his footsteps and I've worked with that brilliant attorney as well.

I was fortunate to have done what I am recommending to you within these pages. With Lee on my team and knowledge of the AIR21 statute we pummeled Delta's dozens of in-house and out-house attorneys. Some might call them 'out of house attorneys,' but my term fits better.

In 2019, the universe brought together an experienced female pilot, who was unwilling to back down, with the most knowledgeable AIR21 attorney at her side, faced off with the most powerful and disingenuous airline in the world who employed one of the largest law firms to represent them, adjudicated by the most highly experienced FAA administrative law judge. I refer to this event as the world championship of poker aviation style.

The stakes were not money, but life, justice, and passenger safety, creating a space where employees are secure to speak openly about safety concerns. I was prepared because I listened and trusted the experience that came to me. I would never have known Lee Seham had Captain Sabel not reached out as he did. I would have never known Sabel, had I not attended ERAU and took his law class. Then I wonder, why did Sabel think of one of his former law students from a year past and reach out when I needed assistance most? We will never know.

During your legal process I assure you that people and experience will come to you. It's your choice to listen. It was your choice to buy this book and regard the information.

Think of the legal process as a scripted play. Your attorney is the director, the witnesses are the actors, and the final brief is the script that your attorney must provide the judge so he or she can see the big picture and all elements. To create this play, you must have a solid foundation as your stage. That prima facie case—solid evidence—is your foundation to success.

DISCLOSURE: I am not an attorney. My advice is based on knowledge learned and firsthand experience. I simply worked closely with, and listened and learned from, AIR21 attorney Lee Seham for five years. He taught me the AIR21 law. I continually learn from him to this day. I have witnessed highly paid attorneys manipulate the law and write false statements. I have observed airline management who perjure themselves in court without recourse, bought-off arbitrators, unions that work with the company instead of defending the employee, dirty doctors who accept payment for a false diagnosis, and a law weighted toward the company. I survived an abusive and unsettling psychiatric evaluation. You will learn from my experience.

This book is not legal advice from an attorney, but everything you need to know before you file a complaint or employ an attorney. This book will prepare you for your battle, if you choose to go that route. It will help you to understand the legal process. It will enable you to question your attorney with substance. This book is a playbook for court that if you follow, you will have a competitive advantage in the legal battlefield, but also an understanding of how to avoid litigation and win without going to court.

The most important aspect of your case, no matter which court you end up in, is that you take control of your life and participate in your case. Know the rules of the game and you can win. This is a guidebook on what you need to know. While focused on the AIR21 statute, this book provides a wealth of information for any litigation beyond AIR21.

Be involved. Participate. Think. Listen. Do not become a victim. Take the bad guys to the mat and stand proud because you did not roll over. If you have the courage to report, you have the courage to persevere. With my blessing to your success, please use the tools in this book for the greater good.

Chapter 1
AIR21
Whistleblower Law Overview

"The purpose of whistleblowing is to expose
secret and wrongful acts by those in power
in order to enable reform."
—*Glenn Greenwald*

AIR21 IS THE Whistleblower law more formally known as The Wendell H. Ford Aviation Investment and Reform Act for the 21st Century (AIR21) 49 U.S.C. §42121. After an employee files his/her charge with OSHA, both the FAA and OSHA independently investigate the complaint. The government enacted this statute to protect employees from retaliation after they reported safety concerns to their employers or the FAA.[2]

Discrimination Law

WHILE THE NAME "Whistleblower" implies that the employee is blowing the whistle on their company to the regulatory agency such as the FAA, this is not necessarily the case. Those who report safety concerns are typically reporting internally to their management team as I did. The AIR21 statute protects these safety advocates. Unfortunately, the law does not protect everyone in aviation, not all reports are protected, and how you report is a critical component. The outline to the requirements on the AIR21 statute follow, beginning with whether the AIR21 statute applies to you. The ensuing chapters will go into greater detail.

Covered Employees

UNDER AIR21, EMPLOYEES of the following types of employers are protected from retaliation for engaging in *certain* protected activities related to aviation safety:

- ☐ Air carriers (holders of an air carrier operating certificate under 49 U.S.C. § 44705)
- ☐ Aircraft manufacturers and designers (holders of type, supplemental type, production, or airworthiness certificates under 49 U.S.C. § 44704)
- ☐ Such entities' contractors performing functions related to aviation safety, subcontractors, and suppliers.[3]

If you checked a box in this list, then this law *may* apply to you. If not, you will engage in a wrongful termination suit if appropriate. This guide, however, will assist anyone in proving their discrimination case, even if the AIR21 law is not applicable, because the preparatory steps are generally applicable to other causes of action. If your management team is gunning for you, or plans to make you the example, this book will also explain how you can protect yourself.

AIR21 is a discrimination law that prohibits discrimination against someone for reporting safety and the reason the complaint is filed with OSHA not the FAA. You do not file an AIR21 with the FAA. I won't say that a third time here, because the explanation comes later.

Statute of Limitations

CURRENTLY THE LAW provides that you must file your claim with OSHA within 90 days of suffering the adverse action.

☐ Were you retaliated against within the past 90 days?

Protected Activity

NOTICE IN THE covered employees' section above, I emphasized "*certain*" protected activities. This is where I have seen many failures in a case because the complaint did not include a "protected" activity. Regardless, *any* complaint you have in aviation *could be* "protected activity" if you were to write the complaint in such a manner to frame it that way. I will explain further in the protected activity section. However, you must meet the protected activity standard, or there is no protection under this law. Not to worry, this is easy if you know how to do it.

Reporting

YOU MUST BRING forth your safety report in *good faith* and prove that management had knowledge of this protected activity, *before* you received retaliation. You don't even need to be correct in your safety concerns, you simply must be objectively reasonable in your belief that it was a violation. I will show you how to frame your safety concerns to ensure you meet protected activity, but also explain how to report and whom you should report to later in this book.

Adverse Action

AN ADVERSE ACTION is retaliation. The best part of this statute is that there are no hard and fast forms of retaliation, leaving this open for the administrative law judge to decide. That subjective opinion might feel scary, but there is a litany of court cases that have identified a variety of ways retaliation may occur, cited as adverse actions, but not listed as examples on the OSHA fact sheet in the Appendix.[4]

While a demotion, cut hours, lack of promotion are examples of retaliation, there are others not listed that judges have found to qualify as an actionable "adverse action." In my case, for example, the judge determined that sending a pilot to a mental health evaluation is an adverse action, yet that's not specifically on the OSHA list. This judge also deemed the surveillance of a railroad foreman in another case as an adverse action.[5] As a general rule, any non-trivial action that would have the effect of chilling an employee from engaging in protected activity may qualify as an adverse action. Were you harmed?

Causal Link

A CAUSAL LINK is the connection between your report and the adverse action. It does not have to be the entire reason so long as it has "contributed" to management's decision to take the adverse action. Just a piece of the puzzle. Even proximity to the time of your reporting, if close to the ensuing retaliation, could meet the causal link requirement. Typically, a few months connection is enough, but up to a year separation could still meet this causal link when considered with other factors.

You will bear the burden of proof until you identify the causal link, and then the burden of proof shifts to the company. At that time the company must prove by clear and convincing evidence that they would have taken the same adverse action against you even in the absence of your protected activity. The good news is, when management has fabricated a pretextual reason, the "clear and convincing" standard is difficult for the employer to satisfy.

Filing a Complaint

IF YOU BELIEVE you satisfy all prima facie elements (protected activity, management knowledge, adverse action, and causal linkage) you should file a complaint with OSHA—the Occupational

Safety and Health Administration. Your complaint must be filed with OSHA in order to protect your employment rights.

What is confusing is that on the FAA website they indicate you can make a safety complaint by contacting their office and filling out an FAA form. Yet, if you read further down on that very same FAA page, they later make it perfectly clear you must file your AIR21 complaint with OSHA, and you only have 90 days to file.[6] Time is not your friend.

The FAA will take no action to protect or defend your employment rights; that is the responsibility of OSHA. The FAA is concerned only with federal aviation regulations.

The Process

YOU WILL FILE a complaint with OSHA who will investigate and rule on your case. Unfortunately, they rarely rule on behalf of the individual and can take years to issue a ruling. The longer this OSHA process takes, win or lose, you can anticipate another 2 years, or longer, for trial and appeal. Therefore, I will explain how to expedite this OSHA process later in this book.

The FAA will become involved once you file a complaint because this is a joint OSHA/FAA investigation. The difference is that the FAA is investigating the regulatory violation, and OSHA is investigating the retaliation. These agencies do not work together and even if the FAA issues a finding that you have reported a violation of federal aviation standards, this determination does not mean that the OSHA investigator will rule in your favor.

More so, the OSHA investigators are public servants and do not necessarily understand aviation safety, or FAA regulatory standards, and they may even lack interviewing skills. At least my OSHA investigator, Paul McDevitt, fit that unfortunate description. During our face-to-face interview, his eyes filled with confusion just prior to pulling a hand over his face. I later listened to two of Paul McDevitt's interviews of management witnesses, both of which identified a company-based agenda, as he put exculpatory words into the interviewee's mouths. Had an attorney been present, they would have cried, "Leading the witness!"

Once OSHA rules, then either side can appeal within thirty days. You will file an appeal with the Office of Administrative Law Judges.[7] Directions for that appeal is at the bottom of the OSHA ruling. I highly recommend an attorney at this phase. With this said, if you've lost your job and now have more time than money, you can file yourself. More on that later. But you must fully understand what it means to be a covered employee first.

Chapter 2
Covered Employees

"If you don't meet the standards,
then you don't qualify"
—Harold Ford, Jr.

THOSE EMPLOYEES COVERED by the statute include those who work for, "Air carriers, manufacturers and such entities' contractors performing functions related to aviation safety, subcontractors, and suppliers."[8]

Aircraft manufacturers were added in 2020 as a result of the MAX crashes, Lion Air Flight 610 on October 29, 2018[9] and Ethiopian Flight 302 on March 10, 2019.[10] In 2020 the *Aircraft Certification Safety and Accountability Act* added the protection of the AIR21 statute to aircraft manufacturing employees during the manufacturing and certification process.[11] Now the discussion on those not covered.

I do not understand why a charter service operating in the federal airspace carrying passengers is exempt to the AIR21 statute, but it is. Or why a fixed base operator (FBO) flight school or a university flight school employee, sanctioned to train your future pilots, do not receive the same protections as airline employees. Especially with joint agreements with airlines and universities and automatic employment opportunities. But this statute does not cover these employees.

However, if you do not qualify for an AIR21 case, you do

have legal remedies when employed with anyone if retaliation occurs for a protected reason.

It's illegal to retaliate against an employee based on considerations of age, gender, ethnicity, religion, and safety. And if the AIR21 is not applicable in your case, a wrongful termination suit may warrant other discrimination laws. Regardless of the rationale as to why your company demoted or terminated you, or sent you to a psychiatric evaluation, you will need facts to prove and win your case.

If the AIR21 statute does not apply, and you are successful in your wrongful termination lawsuit, you may reap a more significant payback than within the bounds of AIR21 law. Currently the AIR21 statute only provides for compensatory damages, not punitive. Juries have the power to award punitive damages in wrongful termination lawsuits as identified below.

> *"A pilot who flew a private plane for Columbia Sussex in Crestview Hills was awarded $1,990,833 in damages by a Boone County jury after he was fired for refusing to fly to the Caribbean as a hurricane threatened. The award includes $1.3 million in punitive damages."*[12]

A word of caution with money as a motivator for your lawsuit. The risk and investment to pursue a case outside the AIR21 statute may not be worth the gamble unless you have a black and white case. Under AIR21, rules are specific. With a jury involved, there is subjective judgment with respect to who is most persuasive in their arguments.

The abovementioned case had a direct connection to saving passenger lives. We fly, we die. Walk away and everyone lives. There was also no argument to the rationale of termination. However, if your case is not as solid as avoiding a thunderstorm followed by termination, jurors may not understand the gravity of the situation and savvy airline management with their highly paid legal team could easily persuade those who lack aviation knowledge to decide otherwise.

I have no doubt that Delta's management team, especially the FAA Administrator, Steve Dickson, could have convinced a jury there was no harm in my situation, and they sent me to a psychiatric evaluation out of an "abundance of caution." The Honorable Judge Scott Morris knew better. Judge Morris is a pilot and had been an FAA prosecuting attorney. Would a jury have his knowledge? I don't think so. But then again, I am also uncertain if *all* ALJ's have the experience and level of understanding that Judge Morris has. I don't think so.

In another instance, a Delta captain owned a side business. Delta employed this captain in the capacity of that other business to participate in an issue on an aircraft of foreign registry, of which Delta was performing maintenance. When the captain, as a contractor, voiced his concern regarding the airworthiness of the foreign aircraft, Delta dug deep into his Delta employee file and fired him for an unrelated reason. Then the captain reported his concerns to the FAA. This captain was not a covered employee because he was not reporting a Delta safety concern as a Delta captain; he was reporting as an independent contractor of an aircraft not of a US registration, and he reported to the FAA *after* the company retaliated against him. He lost his case. He lost his Delta career.

I worked with another pilot at an FBO who voiced training concerns, and the company removed the pilot from the schedule. Despite not being a covered employee under AIR21, we framed a letter with the company's violation of Safety Management Systems (SMS) and risk mitigation, and a settlement ensued without an attorney involved.

> **Note:** SMS is Federal Regulation requiring airline employers to develop a program that encourages employees to report safety concerns that appear to be high-risk in order to mitigate associate risk and improve safety.

Even though this individual did not have the ability to file an AIR21 claim due to *not* being a covered employee under the statute, the same argument would apply in any courtroom. The key is how to write the letter, while identifying regulatory failures. Most aviation businesses have an SMS program, and all flight schools are FAA approved, as are the curriculums. *How you report will provide the leverage.*

On a side note, with respect to the third prong of the *covered employees* definition—*Such entities' contractors performing functions related to aviation safety, subcontractors, and suppliers*—I challenge the breadth as currently applied. The legal question should be whether a university or flight school is a subcontractor, or a supplier providing pilots to airlines and therefore protected. This has yet to be challenged but could be successfully argued.

Furthermore, companies rarely admit retaliatory animus, and often create pretext to make up another reason why they retaliated. Therefore, whichever courtroom you find yourself in, it's important to know *how to* prove your case. You could be right and still lose. You must know both state and federal law. Hopefully with knowledge, you can level the legal playing field.

Note: There are over fifty federal whistleblower statutes, and states have their own laws as well. If you plan to report your company for anything, visit the Office of the Whistleblower OMBUDS and search through their resources.[13] Research your state laws as well.

If you work for an airline or an aircraft manufacturer, the AIR21 statute covers you. Do not allow your 90-day statute of limitations to slip by.

Chapter 3
Statute of Limitations

"Time flies over us, but leaves its shadow behind."
—Nathaniel Hawthorne

"STATUTE OF LIMITATIONS" is the time within which legal proceedings can be brought *after* an event. The event in this case is retaliation. Statute of limitations vary between states, but not within AIR21. Under the AIR21 statute, you must file within 90 days of the retaliation irrespective of where you live.

This brief time limit may become an even greater pitfall when you have a union that says they want to help. The union process could push you beyond your time limit to file, thinking the union is on your team. They may be, but that's not the point. The union won't explain your rights beyond the labor contract, and following their lead could remove all your options.

When Delta sent me to a psychiatric evaluation after my providing a safety report, I began calling attorneys as my union did not appear to be proactive. The company actions in response to my report felt illegal, but ALPA said I had to go through the grievance process. I had no time for a process, my job was on the line. I had never heard of the AIR21 before, but I intuitively knew an employer could not retaliate against someone for reporting safety. Therefore, I took it upon myself to find the information I needed.

Two attorneys told me that I must be terminated before I had a case. Another told me that Delta would either send me to a doctor who would give me a false medical diagnosis or keep me out long enough to fail me in the simulator. The first two attorneys were wrong. Termination is *not* the only type of adverse action recognized under AIR21, but those who are unfamiliar with this law would not know that. Had I waited, I would have lost my case even before it started.

If I had waited until after termination and then claimed the termination was the adverse action (the retaliation), Delta would have claimed they had no choice but to terminate me, because of the doctor's report. They would have been correct. Bipolar pilots cannot hold an FAA medical certificate. By the time they created this diagnosis eleven months had passed since I gave them the safety report. If I tried to backtrack and assert the sending me to the psychiatrist evaluation was the adverse action, then I would have surpassed the 90-day statute of limitations.

I claimed the adverse action was the act of forcing me into a psychiatric evaluation, as the result of providing the safety report. That provided proximity to my report, the reason for my meeting with the investigator, and the rationale that the meeting led to the mental health evaluation. All connected and were within 90 days of my filing.

You must identify the date when your **retaliation** began. What date were you first harmed? That is the time your 90-day clock starts. Adverse actions come in many forms and the occurrence of a new adverse action may re-start the clock with respect to that particular action. A later chapter identifies examples, but you don't need to be on a list to know if management is screwing with you. And until we change the statute of limitations, you have only 90 days from your knowledge of retaliation. If you are pushing the limit, file a charge with OSHA to meet the time limit, and then go back and amend the complaint later for clarity and accuracy. Get it in!

In my case, had I waited to claim retaliation until the Altman report, I *may* have been able to assert that the retaliation was the company's involvement in the doctor's false diagnosis. But only because Dr. Altman provided documents that proved as much. That discovery is something that you should never count on. File when you have felt harmed.

Chapter 4
Protected Activity Defined

*You don't have to be right
if you have a reasonable belief*

DO NOT WASTE your breath attempting to justify why they did what they did, you may never know. And do not assume they won't waste the money to challenge you in court, yes, they will. The only thing you should focus on is if your complaint meets the law by your having reported protected activity.

A little history. In 2017-2018, I surveyed 7491 pilots worldwide for my doctoral research regarding safety culture. Of those pilots, 54% of the population was unsure or did not believe their suggestions for improvements would be taken into consideration, 34% were unsure or unlikely to critique their training program, 41% lacked a belief or were unsure if the leadership in charge of developing training programs had the expertise of learning, 54% were unsure or believed it was best to keep quiet, and 46% were unsure or did not believe their company would exceed regulatory compliance.[14] These responses identify a negative safety culture worldwide.

This is the aviation industry in which we live. Therefore, do not underestimate your management team, or those pilots climbing the ladder, as they will squash you like a bug if they can for their profit or power. My research, now a book, *Normalization of Deviance, a Threat to Aviation Safety*, identifies a negative safety culture and the impact to aviation safety. A negative safety culture is the very reason for the AIR21 statute. This is an industry where management kills the messenger.

Experience teaches that airline management in today's world is corrupt, with profit over safety as the business plan. If you intend to be courageous and speak out regarding safety concerns, prepare yourself for the attack. Arm yourself with knowledge as to what is necessary in your report. And if you live in a kinder and gentler world, your company will thank you for taking the steps outlined in this book. If not, the AIR21 statute will protect you.

You must report *protected activity* to win your AIR21 case. If you do not report protected activity, then you have no case. You may even waste hundreds of thousands of dollars to learn that you never had a case in the first place. Don't go down that path.

What is Protected Activity?

PROTECTED ACTIVITY IS when you provide, or are about to provide, or cause information to be provided to your employer or the Federal Government relating to "*any violation or alleged violation of any order, regulation, or standard of the Federal Aviation Administration (FAA) or any other provision of Federal law relating aviation safety.*"[15] Protected activity also includes if you filed an AIR21 complaint, caused a case to be filed, testified or assisted in a proceeding.

Your report must meet the above protected activity requirement, to qualify for an AIR21 complaint. To ensure protected activity there must be *a violation of a federal regulation, or violation of a federally approved manual, training program, or operations manual.* Any document that the FAA has stamped their approval on is fair game. But, as you will learn in the SMS chapter, you can turn anything that would mitigate risk into protected activity. What you must know is how you report will determine whether you have a case or not.

Framing your complaint
to ensure you have protected activity
is essential.

FOR EXAMPLE, YOUR simulator session was a waste of time. Your instructor didn't know what he was doing. He was argumentative, lacked experience, and to compensate for his shortcomings, he behaved as a bully with the first officer because he had the power. You want to report this training event, but you know that anyone who speaks out against any instructor is made an example of. More so, the director of training hired this guy, and they are buddies. Everyone is warning you that if you report him, they will get you. But you know this instructor is unsafe, he's not training properly, and this is a safety issue, therefore you write the following complaint:

> *"Bob the instructor was being unprofessional, he was acting like an ass, didn't know how to operate the simulator, and I felt he was harder on me than the captain."*

If you were to write anything similar to that statement, and were subsequently retaliated against, your protected activity would be challenged, and you could lose your AIR21 case in a motion to dismiss. Perhaps you could create a case for lack of requisite knowledge, but for the most part it's not illegal to be an unprofessional asshole and your feelings don't matter.

To ensure you protect yourself, you must frame the complaint in the manner to create protected activity. This is an example for the same situation, which identifies without question protected activity.

> *"Bob the instructor was not following our FAA approved training program during the simulator session. He was talking during the sterile cockpit of the LOE and texting in the back of the simulator, both in violation of AQP training standards. He gave me a windshear with an engine seizure on takeoff, when our FAA approved training manual states that I was to have an engine failure with a ten-knot crosswind as he gave the captain."*

You have now identified violations of the company's FAA approved training, violation of AQP, and provided specific examples that contradict the FAA approved training program.

When your airline violates their espoused corporate and ethics policies, legally nobody cares because the FAA does not approve those policies. But any flight operations manuals, company training programs, federal regulations or the SMS policy is open to protected activity because of the FAA's oversight. When you report, use the proper language to ensure protection.

The most important aspect of safety culture is a reporting culture, where employees are both encouraged and rewarded for reporting safety related concerns. Without employees bringing forth safety concerns, there can be no improvement and no mitigating risk. Unfortunately, retaliation is real and creates an environment where employees become fearful to report anything, placing passenger safety at risk.

While it is difficult to understand why an employer would be reticent to accept an idea to improve operational safety, it's as disconcerting to believe they would retaliate simply because the employee provided an internal report. Yet far too often the business decision is to finance silencing employees versus doing the right thing. That's why you must take action to protect yourself *anytime* you report anything. Trust but verify, and always report in a manner that if they come after you, you are protected. The more employees who know how to protect themselves; management may think otherwise before they attack.

It's also important that you understand Federal Regulations, not only for the safety of your flight, but to ensure protection when you report. Your overall knowledge of safety will also help you identify the federal regulation that the company violated in that report. Unbeknownst to me, I had no idea what protected activity was prior to my reporting safety concerns. However, I authored a report of ongoing violations and cited federal regulations regarding SMS and safety culture and therefore met all the requirements. That is not the case for most complainants.

The next few chapters provide a full explanation of safety regulations, SMS, and training regulations, and how to use those laws to protect yourself, with a warning about the ASAP program. These chapters will expand upon protected activity, providing examples that you can use to ensure you, too, have a case with the highest chance to win.

Chapter 5

CRM, AQP, TEM, Safety Culture, and SMS are Protected Activities

"Human history becomes more and more a race between education and catastrophe."
—H. G. Wells

AIRLINE SAFETY IS contingent upon humans. We must identify threats, avoid them, and report to those who have the power to reduce risk. Therefore, the AIR21 statute protects those who take safety seriously and report their concerns.

Applying logic here, if a company intends to retaliate against an employee who reports federal violations, then the company must be violating those very regulations with intent and not by accident. The AIR21 law is in place because the federal government *knows* that airlines and manufacturers are intentionally and willfully violating federal regulations designed to protect the public. Therefore, we all know it's going to happen. The question is whether you will be prepared or not.

Aviation history and federal requirements designed to protect the public will create your AIR21 case and protect you. When you face off with a judge who was an FAA prosecuting attorney, one who understands Federal Regulations, it's best you have your act together. And if your judge lacks understanding in an area, it will be up to you to provide the facts to support your case. This is the very reason you are making your report in the first place—you care about safety.

If you thoroughly understand the history of aviation safety, and the requirements to ensure safety, you will also understand how to draft a report that fits the "protected activity" requirement of the AIR21 statute, or why it does not. Simply stating that something is unsafe, does not always fit the mold as protected activity unless you can tie that safety concern to non-compliance with a federal standard. What follows, if tied to your case, can in fact ensure you have a safety claim.

Pilots receive Crew Resource Management (CRM) and Threat and Error management (TEM) training because the FAA says that will reduce risk. And these programs are FAA approved. Advanced Qualification Program (AQP) is a training methodology that the FAA approved for airlines to reduce expenses, but most pilot do not know all the rules, because there is no requirement to train the pilots as to the elements of AQP.

SMS, however, is a foreign acronym to most employees despite the federal regulation requiring training employees to understand SMS. In that I use SMS in the following CRM and AQP examples, I will provide a simplistic definition here to enable understanding until you reach the SMS chapter.

SMS stands for Safety Management Systems. SMS is threat and error management for the entire company. At Delta, the CEO, not unlike the captain of the aircraft, was the SMS "accountable executive." During my case the company changed that designation, FAA approved, and now the CEO of the airline can designate someone else to be responsible. Overall, SMS federally mandates that all employees should identify and mitigate risk.

You can expect most attorneys to have limited knowledge of these regulations, thus the following information will provide a well-rounded understanding and federal aviation regulatory references they can use to search the law.

Aviation History

IN THE EARLY days, the aviation industry expanded quickly, and airline crashes were due, in part, to under-developed technology, the inability to avoid weather, and a scarceness of ground support systems.[16] Back in the day, aircraft were unsteady, demanded continuous pilot input, and required unyielding attention due to unreliable navigation. As aircraft technology evolved, human factors specialists worked with engineering and flight crews to reduce cockpit workload. Thus, in the early 1970s CRM became the first regulatory mandate to deal with crew interpersonal and communication issues.[17]

Crew Resource Management (CRM) 1990

NOTHING HAPPENS QUICKLY and twenty years later crew resource management, originally termed cockpit resource management, became a movement to teach crewmembers interpersonal and communication skills in effort to reduce pilot error. One of the greatest challenges with CRM was to convince pilots the need to improve their communication skills. The FAA mandated CRM training, and airlines developed programs that were subsequently *forced* upon flight crews.

My first CRM class at America West Airlines, in the early 90's, found many pilots asserting the course was a "touchy-feely" school. Despite resistance from some, CRM took hold and became the way flight crews operated, and CRM became embedded in airline culture. Federal Law required each certificate holder to have an FAA approved training program as identified below.

14 CFR § 135.330 - Crew resource management training.

§ 135.330 Crew resource management training.

(a) Each certificate holder must have an approved crew resource management training program that includes initial and recurrent training. The training program must include at least the following:

(1) Authority of the pilot in command;
(2) Communication processes, decisions, and coordination, to include communication with Air Traffic Control, personnel performing flight locating and other operational functions, and passengers;
(3) Building and maintenance of a flight team;
(4) Workload and time management;
(5) Situational awareness;
(6) Effects of fatigue on performance, avoidance strategies and countermeasures;
(7) Effects of stress and stress reduction strategies; and
(8) Aeronautical decision-making and judgment training tailored to the operator's flight operations and aviation environment.

(b) After March 22, 2013, no certificate holder may use a person as a flight crew member or flight attendant unless that person has completed approved crew resource management initial training with that certificate holder.
(c) For flight crew members and flight attendants, the Administrator, at his or her discretion, may credit crew resource management training completed with that certificate holder before March 22, 2013, toward all or part of the initial CRM training required by this section.
(d) In granting credit for initial CRM training, the Administrator considers training aids, devices, methods and procedures used by the certificate holder in a voluntary CRM program included in a training program required by § 135.341, § 135.345, or § 135.349.[18]

How you use this information can help protect yourself from a corporate attack. Please review the current FAR regulations as they change often. It takes an effort to change a regulation, but when an airline such as Delta places a corporate executive into the position of the FAA administrator or gives an FAA administrator a lucrative board of directors position at their airline, and perhaps financially supports a few lobbyists, the path to quickly modifying regulations may not be beyond reach. Take a photo on your phone, not a company issued device and download with a date.

> **WARNING:** When you are gathering company documents, the safest course of action is to take a photo on your phone. There have been retaliation cases where the company is wrong and did retaliate and lost, but they legally terminated the employee for using company equipment such as a company issued phone or iPad for non-operational and non-approved operations. One such employee was simply watching movies on his iPad on a company work related trip at the end of the business day in a hotel room.

Below is how a pilot can protect himself, or herself as the case may be, if the company decides to make them an example because of their pushback delays. Please remember, that the term "pilot" throughout this book is interchangeable with flight attendant, mechanic, technician, and such, with a variety of situations applicable to the position.

SCENARIO: YOU HAVE pushed back late on your last three flights and management is upset. The chief pilot called you in for a friendly chit chat to discuss this latest event. Word on the line is they are "gunning for you." The company has decided to make you the example.

PROTECTIONS: YOU WILL want to create protected activity *before* you go into that meeting, *prior to* any action the company may take. This means you must write a safety report before that meeting that is applicable to the event.

RECOMMENDATION: ANY AIRLINE or manufacturing employee should write a letter to protect themselves before *any* management meeting regarding any circumstance, be it a pilot, flight attendant or mechanic.

I am reticent to give another negative example, but I believe it's important to distinguish the difference between protected or unprotected letters. The more complaints I have read, I cringe and think... *if only*.

> **Do Not Write:** *"We were delayed because we did not get our release on time, the captain was arguing with the agent to allow non-revs onboard, and everyone was stressed out because the turn was too quick, and it's impossible to meet such demands."*

That statement, or anything similar, would not provide you protected activity.

Frame the exact same situation in the following manner to ensure you will be protected under the AIR21 law, if retaliation ensues after your meeting:

> **Do Write**: *"I am looking forward to meeting with you to discuss my concerns regarding our departure delays. Please know that this delay, not unlike the others this week, was due to conflict regarding operational practices, poor communication processes, and the lack of associated stress reduction strategies, all which conflict with our FAA-approved CRM training program and create a high-risk operation conflicting with the core elements of our FAA approved SMS."*

Author a well-thought-out response that identifies concerns that violate FAA standards and you have created protected activity. CRM training is FAA approved and therefore reporting any practice in conflict with that training will be protected activity. You must do this *before* the adverse action. Therefore, you must write this before the meeting.

An employee could apply this letter to almost any situation on the flightline, be it not following an FAA approved manual or operational practices. It's not unknown that many airlines have different processes in each manual because changes made to one manual don't find their way into the others. This leads to confusion as to which procedure the employee should follow because the company's FAA-approved manuals conflict with each other. If that's the case, reporting this conflict could constituted protected activity if you identify the situation to create a high-risk environment violating SMS risk mitigation strategies.

Advanced Qualification Program (AQP) 2006

CRM MOVED INTO simulator training in the form of the Advanced Qualification Program (AQP), where the FAA combined operational training with interpersonal communication practice. Flight training shifted from training and checking as individuals, to training and checking as a crew. The FAA determined how pilots worked together was more important than their individual performance. Under AQP a captain can obtain type-rating certification during a line-oriented evaluation (LOE) checking event without flying the aircraft. Hard to believe, but that is the law.

AQP provided airlines an economic benefit by granting training departments the ability to reduce the training footprint with a train-to-proficiency concept, notably reducing training expense. At the same time, airlines were required to track crew performance to ascertain training effectiveness, which continues to be a challenge today.[19] AQP also requires the inclusion of CRM training, line-oriented flight training (LOFT), and line operational evaluation (LOE) scenarios.

These training/checking scenarios changed traditional processes where a pilot was trained and checked on individual performance, to a training and checking crew-based, line-oriented, training process. This methodology not only enabled crews to learn how to manage the aircraft, but also worked toward improving team and communication skills. With the availability of exceptionally reliable automated aircraft, designed to reduce workload and improve situation awareness, training departments could now achieve simulator to flight line results quicker than ever before. CRM is an integral component of AQP, and airlines saved millions in training expense.

AQP is a Federal Regulation

IF YOUR AIRLINE trains under AQP, the federal regulation requires the airline to follow their FAA approved training program.

---

14 CFR § 121.909 - Approval of Advanced Qualification Program.

(a) *Approval process.* Application for approval of an AQP curriculum under this subpart is made to the responsible Flight Standards office.

(b) *Approval criteria.* Each AQP must have separate curriculums for indoctrination, qualification, and continuing qualification (including upgrade, transition, and requalification), as specified in §§ 121.911, 121.913, and 121.915. All AQP curriculums must be based on an instructional systems development methodology. This methodology must incorporate a thorough analysis of the certificate holder's operations, aircraft, line environment and job functions. All AQP qualification and continuing qualification curriculums must integrate the training and evaluation of CRM and technical skills and knowledge. An application for approval of an AQP curriculum may be approved if the program meets the following requirements:

(1) The program must meet all the requirements of this subpart.

(2) Each indoctrination, qualification, and continuing qualification AQP, and derivatives must include the following documentation:

   (i) Initial application for AQP.
   (ii) Initial job task listing.
   (iii) Instructional systems development methodology.
   (iv) Qualification standards document.
   (v) Curriculum outline.
   (vi) Implementation and operations plan.

---

(3) Subject to approval by the FAA, certificate holders may elect, where appropriate, to consolidate information about multiple programs within any of the documents referenced in paragraph (b)(2) of this section.

(4) The Qualification Standards Document must indicate specifically the requirements of the parts 61, 63, 65, 121, or 135 of this chapter, as applicable, that would be replaced by an AQP curriculum. If a practical test requirement of parts 61, 63, 65, 121, or 135 of this chapter is replaced by an AQP curriculum, the certificate holder must establish an initial justification, and a continuing process approved by the FAA to show how the AQP curriculum provides an equivalent level of safety for each requirement that is to be replaced.

(c) *Application and transition.* Each certificate holder that applies for one or more advanced qualification curriculums must include as part of its application a proposed transition plan (containing a calendar of events) for moving from its present approved training to the advanced qualification program training.

(d) *Advanced Qualification Program revisions or rescissions of approval.* If after a certificate holder begins training and qualification under an AQP, the FAA finds the certificate holder is not meeting the provisions of its approved AQP, the FAA may require the certificate holder, pursuant to § 121.405(e), to make revisions. Or if otherwise warranted, the FAA may withdraw AQP approval and require the certificate holder to submit and obtain approval for a plan (containing a schedule of events) that the certificate holder must comply with and use to transition to an approved training program under subpart N of this part or under subpart H of part 135 of this chapter, as appropriate. The certificate holder may also voluntarily submit and obtain approval for a plan (containing a schedule of events) to transition to an approved training program under subpart N of this part or under subpart H of part 135 of this chapter, as appropriate.

(e) *Approval by the FAA.* Final approval of an AQP by the FAA indicates the FAA has accepted the justification provided under paragraph (b)(4) of this section and the applicant's initial justification and continuing process establish an equivalent level of safety for each requirement of parts 61, 63, 65, 121, and 135 of this chapter that is being replaced.[20]

If you want to complain about training, identify how *your* training as implemented was in conflict with the airline's FAA approved training program. Be prepared, as your company may change the manuals electronically. Take a photo of the current program. The FAA often changes their requirements without the airline employee's knowledge, unless the employee knew to look for a change.

REMEMBER: EVEN IF the FAA changed regulations midstream, or your company changed policies after retaliation, with the AIR21 statute you do not have to be correct, you simply must reasonably *believe* the situation was a violation.

Note: Appendix F is the traditional methodology of training that some cargo operators still employ. The reporting is exactly the same as with AQP, but specific to the company's FAA-approved training.

Threat and Error Management (TEM)

TEM IS IN essence the fifth generation of CRM, developed to assist pilots with identifying operational threats so they can mitigate risk.[21] TEM began a bold shift to a proactive strategy where pilots assessed their environment, both inside and outside the flight deck, and openly discussed potential threats. It worked. Accepting that errors would occur, and identifying areas of potential threat, created awareness and assisted pilots in anticipating those threats and preparing them mentally for the unexpected event. As pilots trained with TEM, we expanded our flight deck to flight attendants, mechanics, dispatchers, agents, ATC, etc. The more people on the safety team the better.

I suspect your airline's training program includes threat and error management training. Even those briefing slides prior to your simulator session are part of your FAA approved training program. Use them to your benefit.

Safety Culture

LAWS, REGULATIONS, TRAINING, and protections are essential to ensure a positive safety culture. But the reality is, safety culture is still nonexistent at most airlines. The United States Department of Transportation (DOT) safety council identified the most critical elements of a safety culture to be:

- ☐ Leadership is clearly committed to safety.
- ☐ There is open and effective communication across the organization.
- ☐ Employees feel personally responsible for safety.
- ☐ The organization practices continuous learning.
- ☐ There is a safety-conscious work environment.
- ☐ Report systems are clearly defined and non-punitive.
- ☐ Decisions demonstrate that safety is prioritized over competing demands.
- ☐ Mutual trust is fostered between employees and the organization.
- ☐ The organization is fair and consistent in responding to safety concerns.
- ☐ Training and resources are available to support safety.[22]

Safety Culture is the foundation of SMS and will become your best friend in protected activity.

Chapter 6

The All-Governing Protected Activity— Safety Management Systems

"Justice? You get justice in the next world;
in this world you have the law."
—*William Gaddis*

WITH THE NEED to improve safety, the International Civil Aviation Organization (ICAO) introduced the *concept* of Safety Management Systems (SMS) into its annexes in 1980. But it was not until 2015, 35 years later, that the SMS regulation required U.S. passenger and cargo airlines to implement a safety management system, which was to be fully in place as of January 2018.

In 2018, SMS became a federal regulation. Embodied within that standard is a federal requirement mandating a reporting culture and risk mitigation. Therefore, technically, the act of reporting *anything* that will mitigate risk and improve safety should be a protected activity. But only if you frame it that way. This is a new concept to the legal field because SMS is one of the most amorphous regulations I have dealt with since I stepped into an aircraft in 1979.

SMS requires the creation of a program encouraging employees to report **anything** they believe to be high-risk. In effect, under federal regulation, every airline employer should advise their employees if they see something of concern to speak out.

Captain Estabrook lost his AIR21 case against FedEx, in part, because he had reported the manner FedEx was shipping packages was a safety concern. But FedEx was shipping *exactly* as the FAA approved them to do. That did not mean it was safe and not high-risk. Yet, the judge ruled that this complaint was not protected activity for the following reason:

"To be protected activity, the information provided or is attempted to be provided has to relate to a violation or alleged violation of an FAA requirement or any federal law related to air carrier safety, where the employee's belief of a violation is subjectively and objectively reasonable. *Sewarde, supra.* Although a package believed to contain an explosive and later placed on an aircraft seems to indicate a security related matter, Complainant has not established that he subjectively and objectively believed a violation of a federal law related to air carrier safety to have occurred. Complainant may well be correct that the use of combination of package tracking data and aircraft tracking data may allow one to narrow the timeframe of a package's presence on an aircraft, but that alone does not constitute a violation of an FAA requirement or federal law related to air carrier safety."[23]

The judge asserted that FedEx was not violating their FAA approved process, therefore there was no protected activity. That was the understanding at the time, but since my case against Delta the curtain has revealed the wizard. Today we could argue that the protected activity was the violation of SMS and the pilot's duty to identify high-risk behavior. It was the company's responsibility to listen to those suggestions and reduce risk as necessary, not retaliate.

At the time of filing, SMS was not something that the legal system was aware of. Airlines are also violating the SMS regulatory requirement to train their employees; therefore, most employees have no knowledge of this law. I would have had no idea that SMS even existed, had it not been for my doctoral course.

Today, I believe that this judgement would be different if the complaint asserted that FedEx retaliated against Estabrook for suggesting a safer way to package, to prevent the introduction of explosives into its shipments, which is a requirement by SMS to reduce risk. Therefore, the act of retaliation was in response to the act of suggesting a safer manner to reduce risk, a requirement of SMS, not necessarily a violation of how they were shipping.

The FAA has been modifying their requirements since the initial regulation, which appear to be creating more lip service, with an "SMS *department*" that is responsible for everything to include reporting, risk mitigation, and safety promotion, while ignoring the front-line employees. Regardless, SMS intent is to ensure that the entire organization is responsible for safety.

Those personally responsible for safety in an airline operation are the pilots, flight attendants and mechanics. Those responsible for safety are the frontline employees. Without identification of high-risk behavior by these employees, there can be no risk mitigation or safety promotion regardless of an SMS department. There can be no fix without reporting.

Despite the language appearing to focus on the "SMS management team" SMS is nothing without the front-line employees who are free to report high-risk behavior. Anything you do as an airline employee to mitigate risk, as required by SMS, *is* protected activity. However, it's all about how you communicate your concerns.

Do not skim the following regulation. I have interjected notes and examples that you will want to read. The following Federal Regulation requirements for SMS were retrieved from the Code of Federal Regulations on May 24, 2024. As noted at the time of viewing, this information and amendments were published on April 24, 2024.[24]

---

14 CFR Chapter 1 subchapter A part 5
PART 5—SAFETY MANAGEMENT SYSTEMS

Link to an amendment published at 89 FR 33104, Apr. 26, 2024.

Source: 80 FR 1326, Jan. 8, 2015, unless otherwise noted.

Subpart A—General

Amendment published at 89 FR 33104, Apr. 26, 2024.

§ 5.1 Applicability.

(a) A certificate holder under part 119 of this chapter authorized to conduct operations in accordance with the requirements of part 121 of this chapter must have a Safety Management System that meets the requirements of this part and is acceptable to the Administrator by March 9, 2018.

§ 5.3 General requirements.

(a) Any certificate holder required to have a Safety Management System under this part must submit the Safety Management System to the Administrator for acceptance. The SMS must be appropriate to the size, scope, and complexity of the certificate holder's operation and include at least the following components:

(1) Safety policy in accordance with the requirements of subpart B of this part;

(2) Safety risk management in accordance with the requirements of subpart C of this part;

(3) Safety assurance in accordance with the requirements of subpart D of this part; and

(4) Safety promotion in accordance with the requirements of subpart E of this part.

(b) The Safety Management System must be maintained in accordance with the recordkeeping requirements in subpart F of this part.

(c) The Safety Management System must ensure compliance with the relevant regulatory standards in chapter I of Title 14 of the Code of Federal Regulations.

NOTE: Subparagraph C is key verbiage that dictates federal compliance that an SMS must comply with FAA regulations. Any violation of federal regulations violates SMS.

---

14 CFR Chapter 1 subchapter A part 5 *continues...*

§ 5.5 Definitions.

Hazard means a condition that could foreseeably cause or contribute to an aircraft accident as defined in 49 CFR 830.2.

Risk means the composite of predicted severity and likelihood of the potential effect of a hazard.

Risk control means a means to reduce or eliminate the effects of hazards.

Safety assurance means processes within the SMS that function systematically to ensure the performance and effectiveness of safety risk controls and that the organization meets or exceeds its safety objectives through the collection, analysis, and assessment of information.

Safety Management System (SMS) means the formal, top-down, organization-wide approach to managing safety risk and assuring the effectiveness of safety risk controls. It includes systematic procedures, practices, and policies for the management of safety risk.

Safety objective means a measurable goal or desirable outcome related to safety.

Safety performance means realized or actual safety accomplishment relative to the organization's safety objectives.

Safety policy means the certificate holder's documented commitment to safety, which defines its safety objectives and the accountabilities and responsibilities of its employees in regard to safety.

Safety promotion means a combination of training and communication of safety information to support the implementation and operation of an SMS in an organization.

Safety Risk Management means a process within the SMS composed of describing the system, identifying the hazards, and analyzing, assessing and controlling risk.

NOTE: THESE DEFINITIONS are key language. Use this language and associated definitions in your report.

14 CFR Chapter 1 subchapter A part 5 *continues...*

Subpart B—Safety Policy

§ 5.21 Safety policy.

Amendment published at 89 FR 33106, Apr. 26, 2024.

(a) The certificate holder must have a safety policy that includes at least the following:

(1) The safety objectives of the certificate holder.

(2) A commitment of the certificate holder to fulfill the organization's safety objectives.

(3) A clear statement about the provision of the necessary resources for the implementation of the SMS.

(4) A safety reporting policy that defines requirements for employee reporting of safety hazards or issues.

(5) A policy that defines unacceptable behavior and conditions for disciplinary action.

(6) An emergency response plan that provides for the safe transition from normal to emergency operations in accordance with the requirements of § 5.27.

(b) The safety policy must be signed by the accountable executive described in § 5.25.

(c) The safety policy must be documented and communicated throughout] the certificate holder's organization.

(d) The safety policy must be regularly reviewed by the accountable executive to ensure it remains relevant and appropriate to the certificate holder.

NOTE: POTENTIAL VIOLATIONS of your SMS safety policy are likely to include the following and could be utilized in your communications with the company.

- There is no policy for management's unacceptable behavior, and/or not following the policy listed.
- Your company's safety policy was not communicated throughout the organization, because you have never heard of it.

14 CFR Chapter 1 subchapter A part 5 *continues...*

§ 5.23 Safety accountability and authority.

Amendment published at 89 FR 33106, Apr. 26, 2024.

(a) The certificate holder must define accountability for safety within the organization's safety policy for the following individuals:

(1) Accountable executive, as described in § 5.25.

(2) All members of management in regard to developing, implementing, and maintaining SMS processes within their area of responsibility, including, but not limited to:

(i) Hazard identification and safety risk assessment.

(ii) Assuring the effectiveness of safety risk controls.

(iii) Promoting safety as required in subpart E of this part.

(iv) Advising the accountable executive on the performance of the SMS and on any need for improvement.

(3) Employees relative to the certificate holder's safety performance.

(b) The certificate holder must identify the levels of management with the authority to make decisions regarding safety risk acceptance.

NOTE: READ YOUR SMS. Who is your accountable executive? You might want to ensure to copy them on your safety report as well as the entire team.

At the onset of SMS, the CEO was the designated accountable executive. At Delta, that person was CEO Ed Bastian. After VP Jim Graham requested that I give an SMS presentation, I invited Mr. Bastian to join us because of his designation to the SMS program. Bastian turned down the offer, but requested I send him a copy of that presentation. While my invitation and sending Bastian the document infuriated Captain Graham, little did I know that this was an excellent legal tactic for a couple reasons.

Because I had sent emails to Bastian and he responded, and at the time the CEO was the accountable executive, we were able to depose him. But not without a fight. The night before the oral argument with the judge, Lee found an email that Delta inadvertently provided in discovery. I say inadvertent because Delta violated the court order by *not* providing thousands of pages of incriminating evidence, yet within in the thousands of non-bates stamped irrelevant documents that they did provide, we found a couple surprises.

Our process became one of looking for the needle in a haystack. The fact that they were being assholes without bates stamping and info dumping in the final hour, they accidentally transmitted evidence to hang themselves. Buried in the mass were two critical documents. 1) an email sent to Steve Dickson admitting that Graham was planning to send me into a psychiatric evaluation four months *prior to* Delta creating the pretext, and 2) a memo from Ed Bastian to Graham and attorney Peter Carter establishing a March 9th, 30-minute meeting, regarding "Karlene Petitt Update."

My meeting with the purported safety investigator was March 7th and she did not return to Atlanta until midnight, then took the day off on the 8th. Yet, the Bastian meeting update was already in progress before her return.

While Delta withheld most everything of relevance, violating the court order, and provided thousands of un-numbered pages the Friday before our Monday morning meeting with the judge, Lee did what any brilliant attorney would do. He started perusing thousands of pages from *back* to front and found a bullet to win our oral argument with Judge Morris to depose Bastian.

Deposing a CEO is a rare occurrence due to the Apex doctrine because the CEO is typically too high in the organization to have requisite knowledge, and courts are wary of the disruptive impact of subjecting a CEO to depositions. In this case, Bastian's position and interaction with me regarding SMS created his knowledge of my event. Lee found the memo over the weekend prior to our

Monday morning discussion, that Bastian was meeting with an executive and an attorney to discuss me, and provided it to the judge on the day of our argument.

Ira Rosenstein, Delta's attorney, complained to the judge that it was "not fair" to be blindsided by a document in the final hour. Lee said, *"Your honor, I'm a one man show here, and they provide all this discovery late. Besides, how could I 'blindside' him with a document he provided us?"* Which supports my assertion they had no intention of providing it, as they were unaware they had done so.

Rosenstein then complained that Bastian was too busy managing an airline with 50,000 employees. Judge Morris responded that he would like to know why such a busy man was spending 30 minutes with one of those 50,000 employees. We won! We deposed Bastian.

A huge mistake Delta made was not to have Bastian attend the SMS presentation that I had invited him to. Had he attended the meeting, he would have learned that he was the accountable executive, as well as the elements of SMS. With that knowledge, he could have saved himself a great deal of embarrassment at his recorded deposition that is now on YouTube.[25]

During the deposition we learned that he did not know the construct of SMS and he did not believe it was his responsibility to have *any* understanding because he wasn't a pilot or technician. He had no knowledge he was the accountable executive, let alone what an accountable executive was, as he stated. *"I don't even know what accountable executive means."*

Sometime during the legal process, Delta decided to designate someone else as the accountable executive to separate Bastian from the lawsuit, but they did not change that designation in all their documents, and another page identified a "change item" referencing his removal from the position. During his deposition, Lee attempted to elicit testimony of Bastian's understanding of the connection between safety culture and SMS to no avail.

Seham: "You understand that, would you agree that safety culture is a core component of SMS?"

Bastian: "Safety is core to our culture, period."

Seham: "Yes. But that is not my question. The question is would you agree—"

Bastian: "SMS is a tracking vehicle. Culture is about safety. The priority for our airline is about safety."

Seham: "Would you agree that the promotion of safety culture is a core component of SMS?"

Bastian: "I'm not familiar with what SMS includes, but I can tell you that safety is core to the operation of our airline."[26]

If safety were core to the operation, we would not be in trial. Profit appears to be the core over safety. Furthermore, Ed Bastian may not be alone as to the level of ignorance with your management team of federal regulations at the corporate level.

Transmit your safety report to as many people as possible. There is a reason for the chain of command, it protects those above from accountability. But not unlike Delta where all pilots believe there is a chain of command policy, Delta has a written open-door policy. Check your SMS, as you may still have the original version where the CEO is still the accountable executive. Sadly, the FAA allows for delegation of accountability under SMS.

What is even more interesting is that the FAA administrator, Michael Huerta, who enacted SMS, sits on Delta's board, of which Bastian is the chairman. To say there is a breakdown of communication is an understatement.

You should be writing to and or copying any company executives who are required to hold requisite knowledge and have the power to solve whatever problem may exist. Involve those who should be accountable. Involve, your manager, their manager, and take it all the way up the chain to the highest level appropriate. The more the better in AIR21. This implicates the company on every level in every department. Always copy your company's accountable executive.

Open and documented communication will help your case.

---

14 CFR Chapter 1 subchapter A part 5 *continues...*

§ 5.25 Designation and responsibilities of required safety management personnel.

Cross Reference
Published at 89 FR 33106, Apr. 26, 2024.

(a) ***Designation of the accountable executive.*** The certificate holder must identify an accountable executive who, irrespective of other functions, satisfies the following:

(1) Is the final authority over operations authorized to be conducted under the certificate holder's certificate(s).

(2) Controls the financial resources required for the operations to be conducted under the certificate holder's certificate(s).

(3) Controls the human resources required for the operations authorized to be conducted under the certificate holder's certificate(s).

(4) Retains ultimate responsibility for the safety performance of the operations conducted under the certificate holder's certificate.

(b) ***Responsibilities of the accountable executive.*** The accountable executive must accomplish the following:

(1) Ensure that the SMS is properly implemented and performing in all areas of the certificate holder's organization.

(2) Develop and sign the safety policy of the certificate holder.

(3) Communicate the safety policy throughout the certificate holder's organization.

(4) Regularly review the certificate holder's safety policy to ensure it remains relevant and appropriate to the certificate holder.

(5) Regularly review the safety performance of the certificate holder's organization and direct actions necessary to address substandard safety performance in accordance with § 5.75.

NOTE: DOES YOUR accountable executive communicate your safety policy throughout the organization? If not, you could assert in your report that you were unaware of your safety policy regarding the situation because that policy has not been communicated to you, as required by SMS.

---

14 CFR Chapter 1 subchapter A part 5 *continues...*

(c) *Designation of management personnel.* The accountable executive must designate sufficient management personnel who, on behalf of the accountable executive, are responsible for the following:

(1) Coordinate implementation, maintenance, and integration of the SMS throughout the certificate holder's organization.
(2) Facilitate hazard identification and safety risk analysis.
(3) Monitor the effectiveness of safety risk controls.
(4) Ensure safety promotion throughout the certificate holder's organization as required in subpart E of this part.
(5) Regularly report to the accountable executive on the performance of the SMS and on any need for improvement.

§ 5.27 Coordination of emergency response planning.

Cross Reference to an amendment published at 89 FR 33107, Apr. 26, 2024.

Where emergency response procedures are necessary, the certificate holder must develop and the accountable executive must approve as part of the safety policy, an emergency response plan that addresses at least the following:

(a) Delegation of emergency authority throughout the certificate holder's organization;
(b) Assignment of employee responsibilities during the emergency; and
(c) Coordination of the certificate holder's emergency response plans with the emergency response plans of other organizations it must interface with during the provision of its services.

NOTE: As FRONT-LINE employees, you are responsible for flight line emergencies. Do you know what your plan is? If not, you could write this as a concern in your safety complaint.

---

14 CFR Chapter 1 subchapter A part 5 *continues…*
Subpart C—Safety Risk Management

§ 5.51 Applicability.

Cross Reference

Amendment published at 89 FR 33107, Apr. 26, 2024.

A certificate holder must apply safety risk management to the following:

(a) Implementation of new systems.

(b) Revision of existing systems.

(c) Development of operational procedures.

(d) Identification of hazards or ineffective risk controls through the safety assurance processes in subpart D of this part.

SMS is the catch-all regulation to provide protected activity. Safety risk management covers everything under SMS, especially with the requirement for revision of existing systems, and identification of ineffective risk controls. Anything you see that is not mitigating risk or not improving system safety is open for reporting under SMS. Most importantly, if you identify a hazard or ineffective risk control, you report that pursuant to your airline's SMS program because this program reflects federal reporting standards.

Example:

IN THE PREVIOUS FedEx case, the judge ruled that FedEx was not violating their current FAA approved practices because the pilot reported concerns for how they were shipping the cargo, yet the company was following their FAA-approved process. While the judge ruled that forcing this pilot into a mental health evaluation for reporting was in fact unjustified, there was no protected activity that would prohibit retaliatory action under the AIR21 statute. The method of shipment was not an FAA violation. The pilot's complaint, if framed differently, may have survived the protected activity phase.

> *"Dear Chief pilot, Regional Director, and associated managers, the manner in which we are labeling our cargo is impacting safety, because our FAA approved labeling process is making it possible for terrorists to disseminate to the general public where the package is at all times, thereby facilitating detonation time. Under 14 CFR Chapter 1 subchapter A PART 5—SAFETY MANAGEMENT SYSTEMS Subpart C—Safety Risk Management § 5.51 Applicability, we are required to identify ineffective risk controls and revise existing systems. Therefore, I believe we should revise this process to...."*

In the above example, the protected activity is when the pilot identifies a problem and suggests a revision to mitigate risk, as SMS requires. Therefore, with the same event, framing it in a different manner, could identify protected activity. How you write your complaint is the key. This is the very reason companies do not teach SMS, despite the regulatory requirement to do so.

Make it easy for the judge to rule in your favor and provide protected activity wrapped up with a bow.

---

14 CFR Chapter 1 subchapter A part 5 *continues...*

§ 5.53 System analysis and hazard identification.

Cross Reference to an amendment published at 89 FR 33107, Apr. 26, 2024.

(a) When applying safety risk management, the certificate holder must analyze the systems identified in § 5.51. Those system analyses must be used to identify hazards under paragraph (c) of this section, and in developing and implementing risk controls related to the system under § 5.55(c).

(b) In conducting the system analysis, the following information must be considered:

(1) Function and purpose of the system.
(2) The system's operating environment.
(3) An outline of the system's processes and procedures.
(4) The personnel, equipment, and facilities necessary for operation of the system.

(c) The certificate holder must develop and maintain processes to identify hazards within the context of the system analysis.

§ 5.55 Safety risk assessment and control.

Cross Reference to an amendment published at 89 FR 33107, Apr. 26, 2024.

(a) The certificate holder must develop and maintain processes to analyze safety risk associated with the hazards identified in § 5.53(c).

(b) The certificate holder must define a process for conducting risk assessment that allows for the determination of acceptable safety risk.

(c) The certificate holder must develop and maintain processes to develop safety risk controls that are necessary as a result of the safety risk assessment process under paragraph (b) of this section.

(d) The certificate holder must evaluate whether the risk will be acceptable with the proposed safety risk control applied, before the safety risk control is implemented.

§ 5.57 xxx

Cross Reference to an amendment published at 89 FR 33107, Apr. 26, 2024.

Subpart D—Safety Assurance

§ 5.71 Safety performance monitoring and measurement.

Cross Reference. to an amendment published at 89 FR 33107, Apr. 26, 2024.

(a) The certificate holder must develop and maintain processes and systems to acquire data with respect to its operations, products, and services to monitor the safety performance of the organization. These processes and systems must include, at a minimum, the following:

(1) Monitoring of operational processes.

(2) Monitoring of the operational environment to detect changes.

(3) Auditing of operational processes and systems.

(4) Evaluations of the SMS and operational processes and systems.

(5) Investigations of incidents and accidents.

(6) Investigations of reports regarding potential non-compliance with regulatory standards or other safety risk
controls established by the certificate holder through the
safety risk management process established in subpart C
of this part.

(7) *A confidential employee reporting* system in which
employees can report hazards, issues, concerns, occur-
rences, incidents, as well as propose solutions and safety
improvements.

(b) The certificate holder must develop and maintain processes
that analyze the data acquired through the processes and
systems identified under paragraph (a) of this section and any
other relevant data with respect to its operations, products,
and services.

NOTE: §5.71 SAFETY performance monitoring and measurement
(a) (7) a confidential reporting system, is in reference to ASAP. I
do not believe the paragraph as written was in the original SMS
program. SMS must establish an environment for retaliation-free
reporting, therefore why the anonymity? That will be answered
in chapter 7.

WARNING: NEVER rely on anonymity. That anonymity could
result in the loss of your case if management representatives
can plausibly deny the requisite knowledge of your protected
activity. Like pregnancy discrimination, if you are not showing,
you may not be able to prove discrimination.

---

14 CFR Chapter 1 subchapter A part 5 *continues...*

[80 FR 1326, Jan. 8, 2015, as amended at 82 FR 24010, May 25, 2017]

§ 5.73 Safety performance assessment.

Cross Reference to an amendment published at 89 FR 33108, Apr. 26, 2024.

(a) The certificate holder must conduct assessments of its safety performance against its safety objectives, which include reviews by the accountable executive, to:

  (1) Ensure compliance with the safety risk controls established by the certificate holder.

  (2) Evaluate the performance of the SMS.

  (3) Evaluate the effectiveness of the safety risk controls established under § 5.55(c) and identify any ineffective controls.

  (4) Identify changes in the operational environment that may introduce new hazards.

  (5) Identify new hazards.

(b) Upon completion of the assessment, if ineffective controls or new hazards are identified under paragraphs (a)(2) through (5) of this section, the certificate holder must use the safety risk management process described in subpart C of this part.

NOTE. THE PREVIOUS passage is a great section to quote in any complaint. 14 CFR Chapter 1 subchapter A PART 5—SAFETY MANAGEMENT SYSTEMS Subpart § 5.73 Safety performance assessment, (a) (5) "Identify new hazards." If you identify new hazards, you should write up the potential hazard in compliance with this section. The previous FedEx case is a perfect example.

---

14 CFR Chapter 1 subchapter A part 5 *continues...*

§ 5.75 Continuous improvement. Cross Reference to an amendment published at 89 FR 33108, Apr. 26, 2024.

The certificate holder must establish and implement processes to correct safety performance deficiencies identified in the assessments conducted under § 5.73.

Subpart E—Safety Promotion

§ 5.91 Competencies and training.

> *Cross Reference to an amendment published at 89 FR 33108, Apr. 26, 2024.*
> The certificate holder must provide training to each individual identified in § 5.23 to ensure the individuals attain and maintain the competencies necessary to perform their duties relevant to the operation and performance of the SMS.

§ 5.93 Safety communication.

> *Cross Reference to an amendment published at 89 FR 33108, Apr. 26, 2024.*
> The certificate holder must develop and maintain means for communicating safety information that, at a minimum:
> (a) Ensures that employees are aware of the SMS policies, processes, and tools that are relevant to their responsibilities.
> (b) Conveys hazard information relevant to the employee's responsibilities.
> (c) Explains why safety actions have been taken.
> (d) Explains why safety procedures are introduced or changed.

NOTE: § 5.93 Safety communication (a) ensures that employees are aware of the SMS policies, processes, and tools that are relevant to their responsibilities. In the initial SMS regulation, the FAA required airlines to train all employees with respect to SMS. Regardless, this modification ensures employees are only "aware." The question remains as to how many employees have awareness if not trained.

Unfortunately, airlines do not train employees to understand SMS and in some cases ensure they are blind to the law. This regulation is the dirty little secret your management team wants to keep away from you, because all safety concerns and associated reporting can fall within this singular regulation. Therefore, SMS is a secreted regulation that most airline employees are unaware. During my trial, Captain Corbin Walters' testimony spoke volumes:

Seham: Have you ever discussed SMS with other pilots at Delta?

Walters: Well, a little bit. Usually when I say SMS they say: "What is that? Is that part of the airplane?"

Seham: Well, to the extent you have knowledge of SMS, to what do you attribute having obtained that knowledge?

Walters: Because I know Karlene.

Seham: You don't recall any training from Delta on SMS?

Walters: Not that I can recall, certainly nothing extensive.[27]

---

14 CFR Chapter 1 subchapter A part 5 *continues...*
Subpart F—SMS Documentation and Recordkeeping

§ 5.95 SMS documentation.

Cross Reference to an amendment published at 89 FR 33108, Apr. 26, 2024.

The certificate holder must develop and maintain SMS documentation that describes the certificate holder's:

(a) Safety policy.

(b) SMS processes and procedures.

§ 5.97 SMS records.

Cross Reference

Link to an amendment published at 89 FR 33108, Apr. 26, 2024.

(a) The certificate holder must maintain records of outputs of safety risk management processes as described in subpart C of this part. Such records must be retained for as long as the control remains relevant to the operation.

(b) The certificate holder must maintain records of outputs of safety assurance processes as described in subpart D of this part. Such records must be retained for a minimum of 5 years.

(c) The certificate holder must maintain a record of all training provided under § 5.91 for each individual. Such records must be retained for as long as the individual is employed by the certificate holder.

(d) The certificate holder must retain records of all communications provided under § 5.93 for a minimum of 24 consecutive calendar months.

All airlines and aircraft manufacturers must have an SMS, and all SMS policies require employees to report safety concerns to mitigate risk. Therefore, any report made regarding safety concerns could reference SMS standards to ensure those safety concerns are protected activity.

What does your airline's program say? Find your policy and read your airline's SMS. Regardless, even without my knowledge of your company's specific SMS program, I know that risk mitigation is the key that ensures a reporting system. Therefore, *anything* you report to mitigate risk, simply assert that your SMS regulation requires you to take action if you believe operations are high-risk, and the current process conflicts with the federal regulation, SMS. You don't have to know more than that. But, if you want specifics, dig deep and you will find them.

SMS is going to be your best friend before you report. Under SMS, employees must identify threats and communicate those concerns to mitigate the associated risk, in effort to avoid an accident. Somewhat like threat and error management (TEM). But, unlike SMS, TEM is not necessarily a federal regulation, unless your company has an FAA-approved training module that includes TEM. My Delta training included TEM training; therefore, TEM became a federally approved part of training. Crew resource management (CRM), Advanced Qualification Program (AQP) and safety culture can all protect you, if you word your complaint properly, as will SMS. What you should not count on is the ASAP program for protection.

> **WARNING**—airline management, the union, and the FAA alike, will all tout pilots' protection because of an anonymous safety program, Aviation Safety Action Program or ASAP. Do not believe it. I'll explain the ASAP issues in the next chapter.

Chapter 7
Aviation Safety Action Program—ASAP

ASAP is an Oxymoron of Anonymity

ASAP IS A self-reporting program to encourage airline employees to report human error for system improvement without fear of disciplinary action from the FAA. However, the ASAP report is not anonymous, despite all FAA and union propaganda that assert it to be.

> *"The goal of the Aviation Safety Action Program (ASAP) is to enhance aviation safety through the prevention of accidents and incidents. Its focus is to encourage voluntary reporting of safety issues and events that come to the attention of employees of certain certificate holders"*[28]

When airlines assert that they have a "robust" reporting culture because of their ASAP program, they may not have one at all. Retired NTSB investigator Robert Sumwalt says when he hears that a company has a "good safety culture" or that "safety is their top priority" he wants to wave "a BS flag."[29] This was the rationale that Delta touted as to why they had to pull me for a mental health evaluation. Red BS flags flew in the courtroom during trial.

More so, if your company's reporting culture depends upon anonymity, that, too, may reflect a negative safety culture. If the company promotes anonymous reporting, you must ask yourself, *why?* Management should encourage and reward you for identifying situations to improve safety, and if you're anonymous that's not possible.

The effect of an anonymous program is to remove *your* protections under AIR21. In reality nothing is anonymous, and they will know who you are. But, if you write an "anonymous" letter, you have just killed your claim because you can only establish retaliation if management knows who reported. They will know regardless. Don't give them that out.

ASAP Versus Reporting Culture

AN ASAP PROGRAM is a component of a Safety Management System (SMS), but not the Reporting Culture component of Safety Culture required for an SMS. Read that sentence again to fully understand what I said.

The ASAP program became an FAA order (8000.82)[30] on September 3, 2003; whereas SMS became a federal regulation in January 2018.[31] SMS demands a foundation of Safety Culture, to include a reporting culture. However, when the ASAP program became law over 14 years prior to SMS, the program's intent was for pilots to report *themselves* to the FAA with the claim that the errors were unintentional and provide an opportunity to learn from the error and fix the underlying problem that caused it. The theory was, if the FAA did not know who they were, the employees were more apt to report.

During an ASAP discussion at my trial Judge Morris said, *"The program is not accomplishing what it was supposed to. ASAPs are at an all-time high without the fix."* That statement was off the record, shortly after we listened to the testimony of Captain Jim Graham, Senior Vice President of flight operations, bragging that Delta had over 25,000 ASAP reports in 2018, as he touted Delta's reporting culture. Graham believed that the ASAP system was Delta's reporting culture. Yet, a reporting culture relying on anonymity is not a reporting culture at all.

A reporting culture is essential. And to have an authentic reporting culture employees must be free to speak out without hiding. Unfortunately, management doesn't always play fair which is the reason for the AIR21 law. And the very reason the company hides behind the ASAP system, to assert no knowledge due to the anonymity. They know who you are, and that is the reason when you report you must protect yourself from corporate action, even with an ASAP.

While the ASAP program claims to be anonymous, that anonymity is only with the FAA, not your company. Furthermore, if negligence or lack of knowledge become evident, then the FAA may intervene, at which time you do not get a free pass, and your company will provide your name to the regulatory agency. The employee, however, is never anonymous to the company. The ASAP form requests your flight number, date, departure, arrival, and seat position.

Most employees understand that the ASAP program is a get out of jail free card by reporting themselves. However, a Delta manager asserted that this program also enables employees to report management violations. When I first heard of this in 2022, I tried to file an ASAP on a manager, but Delta's algorithm did not work without a flight number and seat position. Reporting an instructor falsifying training records was not possible in the ASAP system.

Management said there was an option to select "other" with both flight number and seat position. Regardless I could not make the system work. Either they have fixed it or not, or it may not even be true. If it is a reality, most employees are unaware of this feature. My caution is against this type of reporting without a follow up.

The fact is, if I had filed an ASAP against the executives who were violating federal regulations instead of boldly giving them a report in person as I did, the company could have taken the same action and claimed anonymity. I could not tie my report to their actions.

The ASAP system does *not* satisfy the SMS mandate of a reporting culture or a safety culture, because of the purported anonymity. Do not count on anonymity and ***do not*** use this method to report anything other than *your* errors. And, if you file an ASAP, ensure you write a follow-up report to your management team. I'll explain why in the next chapter.

Chapter 8
Reporting—Tell Everyone!

"Communication works for those who work at it."
—John Powell

WHEN YOU HAVE a concern, write to your chief pilot, director of training, manager, supervisor and/or senior leader, and copy everyone you can think of who may be involved. The more you invite to the party, the more options you have during discovery and who you can depose, in addition to proving you reported in the first place. Copy your union representatives if you have any.

Writing only to the union does not satisfy the requirement for management knowledge under the law because they are not official company representatives. You might argue they represent the company more than you, but that doesn't matter. Verbal discussions with your union will later result with the following statement, "I do not recall that conversation and we do not record." The union does not count as management, and they have elusive memories. You must notify a manager or supervisor to make your case.

Write concise language that outlines your protected activity and then add the reason you are providing the report. Meaning you care about the safety of our traveling public and that of your fellow employees, and the intent is to mitigate risk and improve safety. This letter should indicate your good faith. Remember, the law says you must report in good faith.

To add to the protected activity claims in the previous chapters you'll see how to write a sentence indicating good faith.

Training Example:

> "Bob the instructor was not following our FAA approved training program during the simulator session. He was talking during the sterile cockpit of the LOE and texting in the back of the simulator, both in violation of AQP training standards. He gave me a windshear with an engine seizure on takeoff, when our FAA approved training manual states that I was to have an engine failure with a ten-knot crosswind as he gave the captain..."

Now add the additional language to identify your good faith:

> "I am bringing this to your attention because pilots are required by law to be trained per our FAA approved manuals and any deviations could send a pilot to the flight line without the requisite training and/ or knowledge, placing passengers in harm's way. Furthermore, an instructor texting, versus paying attention, indicates he is not truly evaluating the pilots. Every pilot wants to know they are safe before they fly."

Delayed Flight Example:

> "I am looking forward to meeting with you to discuss my concerns regarding our departure delays. Please know that this delay, not unlike the others, was due to conflict regarding operational practices, poor communication processes, and the lack of associated stress reduction strategies, all which conflict with our FAA approved CRM training program, and create a high-risk operation conflicting with the core elements of SMS"

Now add the additional language to identify your good faith:

> *"I am bringing this to your attention because highly stressed flight crews who feel rushed not only conflict with our FAA approved CRM training but create a high-stressed environment that increases undue risk, versus mitigating it. Per SMS federal requirements and our very own SMS manual, we are required to reduce risk and that was the very reason my crew slowed down the operation and took the delay. Passenger safety was our highest priority."*

Protect yourself when you file an ASAP

After you write an ASAP use the same methodology to create protected activity and write to your chief pilot, and copy your director of training, direct managers, and union to include the reason you are writing the report to show your good faith. The union is simply a courtesy copy.

Example:

> *"Dear chief pilot, today (date) I filed an ASAP report identifying our crews' missed approach in Haneda (HND). Regardless of the fact that this was not in US airspace, the problem was lack of knowledge of the FAA-approved company procedures for all pilots.*
>
> *One of the "company pages" described in the HND training video is 11-0B and is found in the REF tab in Flight Deck Pro for RJTT. Not under HND. Nobody on our flight crew had seen that page before, and it turns out that there are 13 pages of procedural information there, in addition to the usual pictorial pages for the airport.*
>
> *It appears that ATC can run simultaneous parallel LDA approaches to RWY22 and RWY23, using 1000 feet vertical separation on the intermediate approach segment. Charted missed approach procedures are designed to keep traffic separated during parallel operations.*

> *I am bringing this ASAP report directly to your attention, because this should be immediately rectified to ensure passenger and crew safety. Please find a copy of my ASAP attached. It appears this would fall in lack of information sharing required necessary to mitigate risk per our FAA approved SMS.*
>
> *Without the training department sharing this information, and ensuring all pilots understand these operations, or at the very least they know that they exist and where to find them, we could be headed for a major catastrophe. Thank you very much for addressing this issue to ensure adequate training for all flight crewmembers."*

The above was an actual situation a pilot sent to me. He did provide the information to the training department, because he was a check airman and safe to do so. But that's not always the case. If your organization has a safety culture that is JUST, placing safety first, they will thank you for such a letter. If management has the inclination to kill the messenger, because you made someone look bad, communicating protected activity in good faith in such a manner will protect you. Keep in mind that a report from one in the club is not the same as reporting as a nobody employee. If management believes they know more than you, duck.

REMINDER:

NEVER, NEVER, NEVER, write an anonymous letter to your management team. That will be their defense, claiming they could not possibly have retaliated against you for an anonymous report, because they had no idea you wrote it.

If you write an ASAP, write a follow up report to your managers. If you don't, and your company comes after you and your only argument is because of your ASAP report, the company will claim, "ASAP is anonymous." The company already knows you wrote the ASAP, it is not anonymous, therefore take it one step further with a follow up letter. This suggestion is simply a free insurance policy.

More than protection, if you are writing an ASAP for a failure, like the approach plates mentioned, expediting this information for an immediate solution is far more advantageous and improves safety more expeditiously than allowing a committee who lacks understanding to review it.

On the Hit List

IF YOU KNOW your management team is gunning for you, do not underestimate them using the training department to fail you. During my trial, Lee asked ABC Safety Correspondent, John Nance, "Have you ever witnessed the use of simulator training or are you familiar with the use of simulator training as a retaliatory tool?"

Nance's response was chilling, but not unexpected.

> *"All too often, and I will say, if permitted to, that that's one of the greatest fears of an airline pilot, because there is no pilot, no matter how good, no matter how experienced, who can't be busted on a check ride if somebody wants him."*[32]

If you suspect the hit is on, then write a letter of protection *prior to* attending any training. As employees we know there are dozens of things our airlines do in violation of regulations such as differing procedures from the book to the flight line, manuals not up to date, or something that happened on your last flight. Even scheduling training on the back side of your body clock could be a safety issue. We train like we fly; therefore, if excessively fatigued, through no fault of your own, you should tell those in charge. Write your safety concern *before* you begin training, to have full protection under the AIR21 statute.

If you show up to the first day and realize something is amiss and they are hunting you, or the instructor has a burr up his ass, then after the session write a letter as to what was missing per the FAA approved training program such as a procedures conflict, or training that was in violation of AQP or your appendix F manual.

Mention *anything* the instructor deviated from the FAA approved program. Once again, explain the reason you are bringing this forward, due to your concern for the safety and the necessity that all pilots should receive FAA approved training to ensure safe operations.

Send your letter to as many people as possible, with a management title, the night before you enter the next training session, which is typically the checking event. Director of training, chief pilot, and assistant chief pilot are all a good start. Therefore, if they pull the plug on the checking event, you can claim it was due to your letter.

EEOC protection Versus AIR21

IF YOU ARE an employee and file a complaint with human resources (HR) regarding harassment, gender, ethnicity, religion, or age-related issues, be prepared for anything to happen, because you may end up defending yourself.

The HR department in the airline industry has one purpose only, to protect the company not the employee. In my case Delta management used the HR department to create the rationale to have me removed from duty, because I had provided a safety report. Management told me that I would be meeting with an HR safety inspector, but instead she was the manager of the pass travel complaint department and equal opportunity manager. She authored a false report against me and the company pulled me from duty.

At Delta, HR prohibits pilots from having union representation during meetings. They prohibit any representation whatsoever, and there is no ability to record the meeting. If this ever occurs, take notes, leave the meeting, and immediately write what transpired. Then send the person you met with an email thanking them for the meeting with a recount of the matters discussed. This becomes your record.

If you are to meet with HR regarding *anything*, I recommend you write a report to multiple levels of management, in good faith, identifying protected activity *before* you meet with HR, just as you would before you meet with a manager in your department.

A report involving protected activity, reported to management in good faith, is your protection. If you are operating in a world of justice, with a positive safety culture, you will receive a thank you for writing the safety report, see the necessary changes occur, and nothing will happen other than the meeting.

However, if you shortly thereafter receive an adverse action, then you can file an AIR21 complaint with documented proof of your protected activity and management's knowledge thereof.

If your complaint has nothing to do with safety, and is specifically harassment, gender, age, or religious issues, then you should still protect yourself. I recommend you outline an EEOC complaint and then write to your HR representative, copying your management team, and provide them a copy of the complaint you *intend* to file pending the outcome of your meeting.

The following is a simple letter, with the attached complaint that will protect you.

> *"I am looking forward to our meeting tomorrow to resolve the issues that I have outlined in my attached EEOC complaint. I am looking forward to an expeditious resolution without filing this complaint, if any way possible."*

The expressed intent to file will constitute protected activity if you were to face retaliation after the meeting.

Now a little back tracking. Harassment and discrimination do impact safety. Anyone who is subject to unwanted behavior cannot possibly perform their duties safely when under duress. Therefore, while writing to the HR manager, you could add the following to turn your EEOC complaint into protected activity under AIR21.

> *"The EEOC issues outlined in my complaint also identify high-risk and conflict with our SMS. When people are under duress for any reason, performance degrades. Therefore, it's my federal requirement, under our SMS program, to bring this to your attention to develop a strategy to mitigate risk regarding these events."*

Chapter 9

Adverse Employment Action
and Dirty Doctors

"Corruption is worse than prostitution.
The latter might endanger the morals of an individual, the
former invariably endangers the morals of the entire country."
—Karl Kraus

RETALIATION IS WHAT the law terms an adverse action under the AIR21 statute. The OSHA fact sheet identifies multiple types of adverse actions as listed below; however, the following list is not all inclusive:

- Firing or laying off
- Demoting
- Denying overtime or promotion
- Disciplining
- Denying benefits
- Failure to hire or rehire
- Intimidation or harassment
- Making threats
- Reassignment to a less desirable position or actions affecting promotion prospects
- Reducing pay or hours
- More subtle actions, such as isolating, ostracizing, mocking, or falsely accusing the employee of poor performance

- Blacklisting (intentionally interfering with an employee's ability to obtain future employment)
- Constructive discharge (quitting when an employer makes working conditions intolerable due to the employee's protected activity)
- Reporting the employee to the police or immigration authorities
- Denial of overtime, written warning, anything ["non-trivial" action designed] to intimidate could constitute adverse action.[33]

Do Not Wait Until Termination!

IF MANAGEMENT PLACES a false and damning report into your employee file because you voiced your concerns, that is harm. For example, a negative PRIA record could impact a pilot's career opportunities with another carrier that will read these reports. Forcing a pilot into a psychological evaluation is also an adverse action. This mental health concern is a key tactic for airlines, not only for pilots but flight attendants and mechanics alike.

Retaliation via Mental Health:

A PSYCHOLOGICAL EVALUATION is not necessarily retaliation in of itself, but the rationale and "close" proximity to reporting is the key. This is one of the most widely used methods against airline employees. And for pilots a negative medical evaluation could result in the loss of their medical license and ability to fly anywhere, let alone the company who took action against them.

This is not just a tactic against pilots only. I know far too many mechanics and flight attendants who have faced the same fate. The company can pull *anyone* from the flight line without justification, other than a fabricated story, and *pay* a doctor for a negative evaluation. You may wonder how doctors can legally get away with this, let alone the company, but here is the gotcha.

Courts in several states (including Georgia) have held that examinations conducted at the behest of a third party (i.e., your employer) do not typically entail the establishment of a patient-physician relationship because the intent is to inform the third party, not to treat or diagnose the patient.[34] An employer-appointed doctor, therefore, may owe you no duty of care and may be immune from an action in negligence.

If a doctor that your company requested to evaluate you asserts that you have a mental health issue, and your license is, accordingly, revoked then the company has no option but to remove you from duty permanently. Management will claim it's not their fault, because it was the doctor diagnosed you were unfit to fly, and they had no choice. Why the courts do not look at the price of these false diagnoses is a subject of contention.

In my case Delta paid Dr. Altman $74,000 for a disqualifying diagnosis. Dr. Altman was a third-party doctor, and I could not sue him for malpractice because he worked for Delta. He simply evaluated me, and they paid him. Therefore, there was no physician-patient relationship. After he diagnosed me, I asked for a treatment plan hoping he might reverse that relationship, but he did not provide it. I suspect he knew the law too.

As a side note, Delta paid Dr. Altman as a "vendor," in the manner they pay the guy delivering peanuts. That designation should also be of question. However, after spending three days with Dr. Altman, I fully understand that he was nothing more than a vendor delivering a product. Notwithstanding, he was a nut-job.

In confronting the mental health tactic to remove a pilot, most airline pilot collective bargaining agreements, the contract, have a three-step evaluation process. The company doctor, the employee-selected doctor, and a neutral doctor. In the Delta contract, the neutral doctor was supposed to be selected by the first two doctors. And the company doctor, was supposed to have been agreed upon by AMAS, formerly ALPA Aeromedical, and Delta. None of which happened, but that is another story.

The union was trying to convince me to use Dr. B. as my doctor for the second evaluation. AMAS even said she would read my report for free. However, if Dr. B. had played the same game as Dr. Altman, I could have filed malpractice lawsuit against her, because I paid her for the evaluation, and she would have been my doctor.

I went to the Mayo Clinic instead. Then the company, their attorneys, and Dr. Altman strongly encouraged the Mayo Clinic to agree to send me to Dr. B. as the neutral, doctor. Mayo Clinic refused. However, had the Mayo Clinic agreed to her as the neutral, she would have been evaluating me as an assigned doctor, and there would have been no client patient relationship, and I would have had no recourse.

If you believe a doctor is in cahoots with the company, they probably are. But if they are *your* doctor, you may have legal options available in addition to an AIR21. Contact an attorney. But never fear going to a doctor as "your" doctor if you pay them. Even if the company has financially incentivized them to provide a diagnosis they want, you will have legal action against "your" doctor for malpractice if they render a false diagnosis at the company's request. With respect to false diagnoses rendered by a company-selected doctor, your only option may be to go after the company.

For pilots in the HIMS (pilot alcohol) program, your company may be forcing you to see a specific HIMS AME. Your company may even be reimbursing you for that doctor. But just like a company uniform, you pay for it, you own it, even if the company will reimburse you for it.

If that doctor is prescribing anything, such as a 90-day lockdown as an in-patient, or telling you to see a psychiatrist, these directives arguably engender a physician-patient relationship, and you could file malpractice charges. While I never encourage litigation, these doctors need to be held accountable for their behavior.

At the writing of this book, this patient/client relationship will be tested in a malpractice lawsuit in *Martin Barnard vs. Dr. Alan Kozarsky*, 2024. We shall see what the courts say about the physician-patient relationship when an AME has allegedly acted negligently.

AME Dr. C. made slanderous comments about me and false assertions about my return to Delta on social media. I threatened a defamation suit. He told me that because he wasn't my doctor his malpractice insurance was no good. Not that malpractice covers defamation, it does not. But Dr. C. contacted his homeowner's insurance adjuster because he had an umbrella policy that covered lawsuits. They paid me damages after a 15-minute discussion, on a golf course, with an adjustor. Dr. C. wasn't a mean guy, just stupid enough to write what he did. This doctor has loose lips, and he got his hand slapped.

Regarding Dr. Altman, it took three years, but I finally convinced the Illinois medical board to go after him and he ultimately forfeited his medical license; therefore, he got his face slapped. I tried to sue him, but the courts would not allow me to go after him personally. The greatest quandary is how that man lost his medical license but the people who paid him walk free without any recourse.

I encourage anyone to kick the shit out of a dirty doctor in a court of law for violating the Hippocratic Oath. Medical doctors certifying pilots have the highest responsibility because pilots' health will determine passenger safety. If they are dirty and take money to author a false report, it sounds reasonable they would take money from the highest bidder. God forbid that is the pilot.

Look into the option of fraud if you *relied on false information* to your detriment. Or defamation of character if the doctor provided false information to the FAA and you are subsequently harmed by that action. Those options are available but check for the statute of limitations period in your state.

Identifying a Dirty Doctor and Taking Action

FOLLOW YOUR GUT and avoid those who do not appear on the up and up. For example, I knew nothing of Dr. B., other than word from an American pilot that told me Dr. B. worked closely with Dr. Altman. ALPA was also encouraging me to see Dr. B as my doctor, even *after* Dr. Altman's bipolar diagnosis. Ironically, ALPA wanted me to use Dr. B. as my doctor to counter Dr. Altman. I did a little research and wondered how this woman was qualified for bipolar disorder evaluation based upon her background. She was not. Delta even utilizes an ophthalmologist to evaluate their pilots in the Alcohol program titled HIMS. If the doctor is not qualified for the evaluative subject matter, that should wave a red flag.

Dr. Jon Riccitello with AMAS worked diligently to convince me to use Dr. B. as my doctor, even asserting she would read the 366-page report for "FREE." Who would do that? Instead, I went to the Mayo Clinic.

When we needed that tiebreaker, Dr. Altman fought to make Dr. B. the neutral examiner. These are the red flags I paid attention to during my ordeal, and you should as well. I never used Dr. B., but in hindsight had she been "my" doctor, I could have sued her for malpractice if she had been working with Altman, ALPA, and Delta to provide a false medical diagnosis. At the time, however, I was simply building the strongest case for my mental health and that was the reason I chose the Mayo Clinic.

AME Dr. C. told me that UPS attempted to use him for Captain Doug Green's evaluation and that Doug did not have a mental health issue. That was not the answer UPS wanted, and they found another doctor and Doug lost his job. Apparently at the time, Dr. C. was naïve to the purchasing of doctors. He later told me that he figured out what was happening, and he would "never do that again." Meaning, I presume, help a pilot the company wanted gone.

Dr. C. said, "*This is a dirty business. But it's okay to tell them you're busy, because they don't get mad at you.*" They, being the airline. He also said, "*Doctors can be bought.*" He told me he couldn't be bought but said, "*only my silence can be bought.*" Now if that's not discomforting, I don't know what is.

If the doctor is an AME, file a complaint with the FAA *and* the local medical board. If he or she is not an AME, file a complaint with the local medical board. You must prove malpractice, incompetence, negligence, etc. Research your doctor's requirements for his certification, and if he has violated any standard of care that's what you write in your report. You must articulate the law he or she broke to have a valid claim. But do not forsake your options against the company to go after the doctor. The doctor is the hitman, but the company is paying for the hit.

If your management team retaliated, how do you prove with direct evidence that retaliatory animus was the result of your report? You don't.

Management never admits that grounding or demoting you constituted a retaliatory action. They make up many pretextual reasons for their actions painting you as the villain. Therefore, if they've built a case against you for a demotion, or termination, or even a mental health evaluation you might feel you have a noose around your neck without hope. Do not worry, as I will explain in chapter ten why you don't need direct evidence to prove the entire connection.

HIMS and Retaliation

HIMS, THE HUMAN Intervention Motivation Study, began in 1973 as a research program to analyze alcoholic pilots. Today, this program is one of abuse and impacts aviation safety. There is only one reason the company is offering you an all-expense paid trip to alcohol camp in exchange for signing a contract that you will never drink again. Your signature on that contract releases your life to the management team, and they own you, control you, and will remove you from duty at their whim.

If you do not have the ability to show up sober to work, then get help. You do not need or want the company to manage your health in *any* manner because they will control your life and will make it hell. In this program you are prohibited from having a glass of Champagne at your daughter's wedding, and if you eat the wrong food before a blood test it could be the end of your career. The hoops you jump through daily will impact your free time away from work and damage your relationships.

This program places a proverbial rope around your neck that at any time you look crosswise at someone of influence, call in sick too often, report safety, or tell them you will not fly fatigued, they will kick the horse on which you sit. Your end will be imminent.

The misconception that the HIMS program saves pilots careers is wrong. Airlines have terminated more pilots in the program, without drinking, than anyone flying after alcohol consumption. Where is the union help? Well, here is the gotcha.

Pilots who argue or fight with a management pilot, fall on a layover causing the delay of a flight, or request a follow-up for the safety report they filed, the union will tell them to go into the HIMS program to avoid termination. Even if the pilot did nothing wrong, and with the union's knowledge that the pilot doesn't drink alcohol, the union will still promote the program. It sounds like the union is working with the company to the pilot's demise, but the truth is HIMS is an ALPA Profit Center.

The HIMS program does not require alcohol consumption to join. ALPA touts the program as a pilot's "get out of jail free" card. Ironically, this is the program that puts the pilot into jail and locks them in a cage for the remainder of their career. Logic questions why an airline will pay for and allow a pilot to go into an alcohol program when a pilot doesn't drink. The answer is, this is the first step in removing the pilot from their career.

This program is a huge business, and the company owned doctors believe they have free rein to do whatever they want and make a lot of money doing the company's bidding. A recent legal filing alleges that Delta's preferred ophthalmologist AME falsely reported Captain Martin Barnard to the FAA for drinking, when all his highly sensitive biomarker tests indicated otherwise. That legal battle continues, and Marty is willing to talk to and support anyone involved in HIMS or planning to enter the program.[35]

Captain Mike Danford, a former Delta pilot, lost his job because, despite the fact he did not drink, he received a false positive. He attempted to fight it instead of returning to a program that consumed his life and conflicted with his beliefs. During a grievance hearing, despite a preponderance of evidence that false positives do exist, the arbitrator said that there were no "peer reviewed journal articles," therefore the arbitrator would not accept that the blood test was false, despite all the comparative tests and data that proved he did not drink. Mike is willing to speak to anyone regarding this program and offers his assistance.[36]

False positives do exist, and if you are someone fighting a false positive, you can access that data from my research *PEth Testing False Positives*.[37]

Your only requirement as a pilot who receives a DUI is to report it to your AME and follow the FAA guidelines for a special issuance. Federal law *does not* require you to enter a company-sponsored HIMS program. A United Airlines pilot proved just that.

My opinion: Don't drink and fly, and never go into the HIMS program.

Chapter 10
Causal Link

"It is a mistake to look too far ahead. Only one link of the chain of destiny can be handled at a time."
—Winston Churchill

ONCE YOU FILE an AIR21 complaint you have the burden of proof "until" you identify a causal link between your safety report and the ensuing retaliation. This link could be temporal proximity, meaning the retaliation was close to the reporting. It could also be action taken by the company in response to something they learned during an investigation of your report. Shifting company rationales or even withholding the purported rationale of the adverse action from the employee could also determine that connection too.

Prior to my trial with Delta, I established that I reported protected activity in good faith to senior management and they retaliated. And the judge had already claimed a forced psychiatric evaluation was an adverse action in another case. Therefore, we spent nine days in trial on causation—an effort to prove what they did was the result of my report.

The company argued against the admission of my complaint and safety concerns during the opening statements when Ira, Delta's attorney, stated, "And we should start, really, by pointing out what you, Your Honor, stated at the onset of this case. We've stipulated that Complainant engaged in protected activity under the statute when she made her report to Captain Graham and Captain Dickson on January 28th, 2016, a little over three years ago.

"So, this hearing should not be about grinding through the specific safety related issues that she raised in that document. Delta has never contested—never contested—that Complainant raised those issues, for any reason other than that she, herself, is concerned about safety—as she should be."[38]

Ira misled the judge regarding this fact. But how could a judge remember an ongoing battle of one event, when dealing with so many cases? I suspect this was what Ira counted on, and I wonder if Judge Morris did remember Delta's arguments and battles before they agreed to the protected activity. It was just before trial began when they finally stipulated to the fact that I had engaged in protected activity, and even the judge had commented that it didn't matter if they had or not, because he had reached his own conclusion that I had met the standard.

Regardless of Ira's pleas, the judge allowed us to present all the evidence and grind through the safety events. This is exactly what you will want to do in your case. If you end up in trial, you will want *everything* in front of the judge, as that is the only way he or she will understand the gravity of the situation. Not that the severity of the safety lapse is an element of the law, but a full understanding of what is at stake is essential to encourage the judge to throw the book at the management team playing with passengers' lives.

The problem is, nothing ever happens to the people engaged in the injurious behavior, as the law only allows to name the company in the lawsuit, not individuals. Therefore, there is no management accountability. This is one of the points in the government accountability project to change the AIR21 statute, as outlined in chapter 18. Until that change arrives, we can only hold the airline accountable, and to do that you need a causal link.

In that judges know that employers are rarely stupid enough to put into writing that they retaliated in response to your report, temporal proximity becomes your best friend. With most cases that proximity is within two to three months. However, the ARB has relied on the ALJ's analysis, which framed the issue of temporal proximity in terms of whether the protected activity had occurred within "one year" of the adverse action:

> *Although the ALJ credited Clark with numerous protected activities, only three of those acts occurred within a year of his June 26, 2002, dismissal. The ALJ found Clark's October 2001 Hotline complaint and two February 2002 complaints regarding a duty-time violation and alteration of the Flight Standards Manual to be sufficiently close in time to the June 26, 2002, dismissal to raise an inference of discrimination. Clark at 13 (emphasis supplied) (footnote omitted). Thus, the ALJ found that protected activities occurring as much as* **four and even eight months** *before the adverse action were "sufficiently close in time" to raise an inference of discrimination.[39]*

You may only need one connection to proceed. In my case, however, we captured Delta every way possible. First, I had established temporal proximity because Delta placed me into a psychiatric evaluation within two months of my presenting the safety report. Second, I had met with Kelly Nabors, the manager of the pass travel complaint department, alias HR safety investigator, on the premise that she was investigating my safety report. The report in entirety sat on the table and she took notes on it, clearly a connection.

Captain Graham had advised me that I was meeting with a safety investigator as they were taking my concerns seriously. Delta later asserted this was an Equal Opportunity investigation into gender discrimination, but that falsity was not pertinent, as a matter of law, in an AIR21 case.

What I learned is that the legal process overlooks untruths. The company will throw irrelevant shit at the wall. You need to duck, ignore it, and just prove the truth of legal facts and go forth. Those who lie will continue to do so. Don't be one of them.

The fact that Delta misled me as to the intent of the meeting did not matter. Nor did the misrepresentation as to the rationale for the meeting. Not even the fact that Nabor's was not an HR safety investigator and had no experience investigating pilot issues mattered. Granted, Ms. Nabors' false assertions of my emotional upset at our meeting compared to the Judge's observation of me in court flagged concern, and he later challenged her credibility. However, to establish my case we simply had to show that my report led to the adverse action.

My report was the "reason" for the meeting. Since my forced psychiatric evaluation was the result of that meeting, we established the nexus. The connection. Without a meeting regarding my report, Nabors could never have asserted I was emotional and paranoid.

During trial SVP James Graham was guilty of shifting rationale. He told one elaborate story during his deposition and then another diametrically opposed story during the trial. The judge asserted that he lacked credibility. A polite way of saying he appeared to have lied under oath. But perjury charges never ensued, because nobody in the legal system cared. But if you lie as an employee, I highly suspect that will be the reason for your loss. The company has nothing to lose by lying, falsifying records, and perjuring themselves. This is a major difference in the power structure.

Also, if your company withholds the reason for your demotion or termination, that will support an inference of retaliatory animus. Delta withheld the reason why they were sending me to a psychiatric evaluation for nine months. It was Dr. Altman's medical report that provided me the reason for the initiation of the compulsory psychiatric examination. I had no idea I cried for three hours in a hotel lobby discussing my report.

You have the burden of proof that your report was, *in part*, the reason for the retaliation. You *do not* have to show it was the *primary* reason, but only a *contributing* factor. Once you show your protected activity was a contributing factor the burden of proof shifts to the employer. When the burden shifts, the company must prove, by clear and convincing evidence, that they would have taken the same action regardless of the report. Granted I covered causation in every area, but you do not have to. Temporal proximity could establish a connection.

If you can establish that you engaged in protected activity by reporting safety lapses in good faith to management and subsequently received retaliation, you have 90 days from the date of the adverse action to file your charge with OSHA. How to do that will follow in the next chapter.

Chapter 11
Filing the Complaint

"Knowledge is a good thing.
The promotion of ignorance is a tool of those
who want to control others."
—Lee Seham

MY ADVICE IS to engage an attorney. But you could do this on your own if you choose. You (or your attorney) will file your complaint on the OSHA website. This is an OSHA complaint. If you find yourself on an FAA whistleblower page *do not* follow the link to file with the FAA. Use the link to file with OSHA at the bottom of the page.[40] My suggestion is to go directly to the OSHA page under how to file a Whistleblower complaint so there is no confusion.[41]

File the complaint to ensure you have met your 90-day statute of limitations period. You can always amend it later. Then write to all your supervisors and tell them that you filed a complaint and why. This will protect you from further retaliation. Retaliating against someone who has filed an AIR21 complaint is prohibited under federal law.

Retaliating against anyone for filing an EEOC complaint, or any complaint with the state or federal government is against the law. After you file, send a copy of your complaint to management and your supervisor, to let them know what you filed, to protect yourself. They will soon learn, but this early notice protects you if any retaliation ensues as a result.

The Process

1. File a complaint on the OSHA website within 90 days of the adverse employment action.
2. An OSHA investigator will contact you and request further information and documents. I met with this investigator and learned that OSHA should never be involved in an aviation safety investigation. That is another book unto itself. But they do not understand aviation safety.
3. This is a joint FAA/OSHA investigation. Therefore, at the same time OSHA is investigating the employment discrimination issue, the FAA should be investigating safety concerns in the report. In my case, the FAA found Delta in violation of a duty time regulation, but that did not matter to OSHA or change the outcome of the OSHA investigation.
4. What many attorneys do not understand is that you can either pursue an OSHA investigation or request a dismissal which means you take the loss at the OSHA level. But that dismissal provides you the right to immediately appeal and go directly to the judge. Lee Seham uses this "take a loss" as workaround because OSHA can take years to finish an investigation and when you're unemployed, you should not be twisting in the wind waiting for an incompetent investigation. Furthermore, OSHA typically rules in the airline's favor.
5. When OSHA dismisses the case, the OSHA investigator will provide you a document detailing the reason for the dismissal and how to file an appeal. They will also provide this information if you take the loss. Upon receiving an OSHA dismissal letter, you have 30 days to file for an appeal with the Office of Administrative Law Judges—OALJ.
6. The OALJ will assign a judge to your case.
7. While waiting for the assignment of your judge, you have work to do as you prepare for discovery, e.g., interrogatories, document requests, and notices of depositions.

8. If the company fails to respond to your discovery request, you may file a motion to compel, which is a formal request to the Court to order the airline to comply with a discovery request such as a request for production of documents, requests for admissions, interrogatories, and subpoenas as appropriate.

9. You should consult an attorney for assistance with the document request. You can also expect the company to write a motion to dismiss, and you will need a cogent reply. If this is an airline, they frequently argue that the Railway Labor Act (RLA) requires pilots to adjudicate their claims via the grievance process. This is where you must understand AIR21 and that the law allows you to avoid the grievance process when safety is involved, and you are not seeking an interpretation of your collective bargaining agreement. More on that later.

10. The judge will make the decision on your Motion to Compel.

11. You can expect a pre-trial teleconference, which will outline dates for ensuing actions and trial.

12. Your company should answer your discovery request, but in Delta's case that was a fight. They delayed, and we had to force the issue with the tribunal. But at the end of the day, our priceless discovery came from Dr. Altman. All of which originated from Delta to Altman in the form of emails and a binder shipped to Dr. Altman for a covert, 10.5-hour, hotel meeting in Chicago, with the doctor, Delta's Labor Relations attorney Chris Puckett, and chief pilot regional director at the time Phil Davis. But, in their discovery responses, Delta did not provide these critical documents that it transmitted to Altman as part of the compulsory psychiatric examination process. If you deal with dishonest people who believe they are more powerful than the legal system, you have your work cut out. Just know that the company will fight discovery, because they are rarely, if ever, held accountable.

13. You will answer their discovery request.

In reference to the motion to dismiss, you can expect your airline to file this motion based upon preemption. Meaning they tell the court that the airline has a labor contract, and these simple disputes belong in the grievance process. There are many reasons to file a motion to dismiss, such as an action being time barred or not meeting the elements of the law and such, but preemption appears to be the airline's favorite tactic when they know they cannot win in the courtroom. Sadly, "airplane court" under the RLA is the grievance hearing, and nothing short of a kangaroo court.

The RLA and Grievance Process.

THE RAILWAY LABOR Act (RLA) is an Archaic Law formed in 1926 governing railroad workers and then subsequently airline employees. This is where special bargaining dispute resolution procedures apply to railways and airlines. The National Mediation Board ("NMB"), an independent Federal agency, oversees the RLA. This does not serve employees well.

If you have a claim that is based on an *interpretation* of the collective bargaining agreement that the company disputes, the judge will throw it back to the grievance process. However, Judges have jurisdiction over issues arising under AIR21; not your labor contract, not the RLA. But federal court is not where the airline wants to be, as they don't have as much control as they do in arbitration.

If you file an AIR21, expect the company to fight to keep your complaint in the arbitration process. A grievance hearing is a legal proceeding in which the airline has the ability to proceed *without* providing discovery. If you have received formal discipline (e.g. a suspension without pay or termination) it may benefit you to proceed with *both* a grievance arbitration and AIR21 action on parallel tracks because the AIR21 affords you discovery rights. Whereas, under a union contract, the company has the burden of proving that any formal disciplinary action taken was with "just cause."

The AIR21 law focuses on whether your safety report "contributed to" the adverse action you have suffered. By contrast, the arbitral process focuses on whether the disciplinary action was fair or just. If you are a non-union employee, the AIR21 route may be your only option. Personally, I would stay away from the grievance process if my career was on the line. If the airline wants you gone, you will not win your grievance even if you should.

While Lee told me he's had numerous victories in arbitration where the union was on his side, I have witnessed the purchase of arbitrators. The good news is you can file both an AIR21 complaint and a grievance. If you do however, plan for a collateral stopple claim against you when you lose the grievance, asserting that you cannot try the same issue twice. Therefore, be extremely clear that one is a contract violation, and the other is retaliation for reporting safety.

Delta filed motions arguing preemption in my case trying to move this into the grievance process instead of Federal court. But during an oral argument, Judge Morris said, "I don't need to know your labor contract to know that forcing a pilot into a psychiatric evaluation is retaliation."

The airline claimed that my mental health evaluation fell under Section 15 of our contract and therefore belonged in a grievance process. Yet AIR21 creates rights under federal law not provided for in the contract. Semantics are critical and this is where an attorney who understands both the RLA and AIR21 will be of immense value.

During the arbitration process the airline and union are joint parties in the action, with arbitrators selected and compensated by both the airline and the union. The grievant involved in this process will have their cases adjudicated by arbitrators who are businessmen in a constant search of their next contract.

In the arbitration process, rulings become a business decision and the grievant can expect a measure of rough justice. When the airline wants to win, and the union is ambivalent, the chances are that the company will win regardless of the evidence. The businessman, called the arbitrator, is *heavily* influenced by which party—the company or the union—cares more about the case. If your union is not providing you full support, it is very likely that the win goes to the company. This is not an assumption, but fact based upon experience.

Safety-related decisions that impact federal aviation standards should be in hands of federal administrative law judges, not in the hands of a businessman, which is the rationale underlying Congress' enactment of the AIR21 statute.

Opposing a company's motion to dismiss might require an attorney, at least for this stage, unless you fully understand your rights and the AIR21 statute and have the ability to articulately communicate in writing.

My advice is to find and allow an attorney to help you. But remember, they are not all created equal. The next chapter will explain what to look for in an attorney.

Chapter 12

Finding an Attorney

"Don't dwell on what went wrong.
Instead, focus on what to do next.
Spend your energies on moving forward
toward finding the answer."
—Denis Waitley

ALL ATTORNEYS ARE not created equal. My first attorney advertised he was an AIR21 attorney. The first red flag was that he filed my complaint without allowing me to read it prior to filing. He provided me a copy *after* he filed, at which time I learned that he named American Airlines instead of Delta.

He also charged me $3500 to tell me that I could not fly with a bipolar diagnosis. Livid, I explained, "I already know that! I could have told you. An eight-year-old could have done a ten-minute google search and found that information." He assured me that I would get all my attorney fees back when I won. He was wrong, but at the time I believed him. And what if the Complainant loses? They are stuck with these exorbitant fees. A law license should not be a license to steal.

After a year of floundering and writing checks for his $500 per hour fee, my ERAU law professor called to see how I was doing. I explained my concerns with my attorney, and that another law firm wanted my case if I dropped the safety claim. He recommended I speak to Lee Seham. I paid Lee for an hour to discuss my case and answer my questions. This is when I learned that I would *not* get all my attorney fees back even if I prevailed. Lee explained the law, and then he sent me a case that he had just lost so I could read the judge's ruling.

I immediately texted my attorney and asked if I could see all his AIR21 cases. Seconds later the phone rang. That's when he disclosed that he had never done an AIR21 case before, but asserted that he had been before an ALJ, and the AIR21 portion did not matter. He was wrong. Yes, it did matter, as it will in *any* AIR21 case.

This is a unique law, and experience is essential because the rules are different than any other whistleblower case. This attorney did not know about the reasonable legal fees, and his assumptions could have cost me dearly. Had I stayed with him, I'm not sure if I would have prevailed. And if I had succeeded, my award would not have covered his fees. I would have won but lost.

I fired my first attorney and employed Lee Seham. Lee read the initial complaint and Delta's response and identified the first of what would be many false statements from Delta's legal team. Delta inaccurately cited a Northwest Airlines case and asserted that the airline won. This was not true.

My first attorney never questioned that assertion, and therefore why would the judge? When Lee saw mention of this case, he had familiarity with it and knew the pilot prevailed, not the airline. An attorney with AIR21 experience and knowledge is essential not only for case history, but for his or her ability to meet the standards outlined within the statute. Equally so, they need to have the ability to communicate effectively.

Writing Skills

LEGAL PROCEEDINGS ARE 95% about the written word. If your attorney lacks writing skills, you will be paying two or three times as much for a lesser product. I learned early that Lee could rough out a first draft brief, written better than the final complaint of my original attorney.

An attorney with knowledge of the law, an understanding of the events, and possessing a way with language will not only increase your chances of winning your case but will enable you to keep your fees as low as possible. Ask if your attorney has ever done an AIR21 case before, and if not determine how much they know about this law. When they tell you -they have done many whistleblower cases, ask how many were AIR21.

There is always a first time for everything, and you could provide them this book for understanding of the AIR21 statute. However, when you are interviewing an attorney tell them about your case, and then ask the attorney to write a paragraph on how you meet the elements of the law or what they believe your case to be. You will learn if they listened, if they understood your case, but also whether they have the ability to articulate your situation in a reasonable amount of time with clear and precise language. You are assessing their writing skill. If they can't do this, you might want to look further.

Contingency

EVERYONE WANTS AN attorney to take their case on contingency. But the problem is that this law only awards "reasonable" attorney fees if you win, which could be substantially less than you may spend if a judge determines that charges were not "reasonable." In my case, Delta engaged in a war of attrition to run my attorney fees higher than the typical compensatory damages. My case spanned seven years. In that this law only allows for compensatory damages (not punitive) and not 100% attorney fees, no individual attorney could work for free for close to seven years and "maybe" receive a portion of payment for their time spent.

Until we change the law and allow for punitive damages, more than likely you will be financing your AIR21 attorney out of your pocket.

I know of cases where attorneys have told the employee they have done whistleblower cases before and will take their case on a contingency. But these are not AIR21 whistleblower cases, which are a different animal. These attorneys do not file at the outset but write a demand letter thinking that the company will settle, and they can earn a quick 30-40% from their demand, if successful. That's not how airlines work. They don't typically settle without a fight.

The company will drag this negotiation process out as long as possible. More than likely by the time you find an attorney you have killed two months. Letter writing, the response and a reply take time. I know of one case that a pilot fell into this trap, despite hours of explanation. He then exceeded his statute of limitations. In another case, the attorney had no other clients, so why not? I spent hours on the phone explaining the law to that attorney. I'm uncertain if he listened. The ruling will be out soon.

Another whistleblower attorney, involved in the rewriting of the AIR21 statute we are hoping to pass, recommended a change that would enable the employee to use the grievance process for reporting safety. First, this option is already available under the statute and if used, the employee could lose all their discovery rights and their career. Second the AIR21 statute became law to remove safety from businessmen rulings in the grievance process. While a highly experienced whistleblower attorney, he had no knowledge of these facts or the statute.

When you are under duress from the company, lost your job, or sent to a Soviet Union style psychiatric evaluation, you want to believe that someone will help you for free. Yet, nothing in life is free. And in this instance, the attorney may not understand the AIR21 statute if they take your case on contingency.

If you need an attorney on contingency your best bet, for *any* legal action, is to contact a large law firm with a couple hundred attorneys on staff. Those are the entities that can afford to accept cases on contingency, as their other cases float the expense of yours. But they more than likely will have limited AIR21 experience if any. You will have to lead the process and explain the law.

When I was floundering with my original attorney, another attorney heard of my case through a fellow pilot dealing with a different legal action in their law firm. This attorney's firm wanted my case and stated they would take it on full contingency, but only if I dropped the safety aspect. This was when Captain John Sabel called and connected me with Lee.

During my initial discussion, Lee advised me that I could file both cases—sexual discrimination and AIR21—because they are not mutually exclusive. The company may not have tolerance for a woman who tells them what to do versus a man. Which was more than likely the case with me and Captain James Graham. A check airman told me that Graham hated three things: (1) female pilots, (2) Northwest Airlines pilots and (3) anyone telling him what to do. True or not, I fit all three categories. Regardless, my concern was always about safety.

Ironically, during trial we learned Delta had converted my safety concerns into a gender investigation, which would have nailed them in a gender discrimination suit because they never followed through and finished the alleged investigation. The EO pass travel manager, Kelley Nabors, dropped the alleged gender investigation the day she provided her report to Delta. This was a report written in part by the labor relations attorney Chris Puckett, who was not at our meeting.

Puckett however provided answers to questions he tasked Nabors to ask me at our meeting, before I ever met with her. One can learn all sorts of fun tidbits in discovery if you look. Nabors did not have time to assign and/or finish the report because of her promotion a month later, as I began my fight to return to duty.

Legal Assistance

I EMPLOYED LEE and he invited me to work with him, which enabled me to keep my fees lower. He taught me the law, allowed me to edit briefs, and review case law. A friend of mine filed Pro Se, and Lee held this pilot's hand throughout the process ensuring all documents were in order. If you're not employed and have the aptitude to conduct research, you could do it. But I suggest you get an attorney to either do the entire process or assist you with the more challenging parts.

If you desire ultimate success and have the tendency to be the captain of your life, you will want to participate in and understand the process. Find a law firm that specializes in AIR21 cases, values your aviation experience, and appreciates input with respect to your company policies, rules, and regulations.

If you develop a "work together" relationship, voice your opinion on what you know to be true regarding events and aviation safety, but accept the legal acumen of your attorney. I track-changed Lee's documents so he could readily see my input, take what worked, reword content he wanted to keep, and delete what was not useful. He was always the final authority on the law because I trusted him. You must have trust in your attorney.

Trust But Verify

AFTER I RETURNED to work, I flew with a former union representative who left his ALPA position due to politics. He asked how I knew ALPA was not supporting me, and how to know what to rely on and what not to believe. I explained that I trusted but verified everything. When something was illogical, I challenged it. Common sense, while not common, can be your best friend when your career is hanging by a thread while determining who to trust. Do not dump your life in someone else's hands. You take control and guide that ship.

Legal BS

THE BULLSHIT CAME from the other side of the courtroom. The lies and misconstrued facts in briefs were nothing but attorneys being "zealous" advocates for their client. Beware, when you employ any attorney who is in the legal business for money, they only focus is on billable hours. That was my first attorney. They have no skin in the game. However, there are attorneys who love the law, inspire truth and justice, and the goal is to achieve success for the right reasons with honesty. Lee Seham and his partner Samuel Seham are two such attorneys, as is the culture of their entire law firm.

The truth of the matter is, that the legal system does not defend right and wrong; the system enforces the law, whether the result is right or wrong. Find an attorney who understands this. Your case must satisfy the applicable legal standards to win. And when you do, there are remedies. At the time of writing this, those remedies are not what they should be. However, if you get your job back, that is a win.

Chapter 13
Remedies

*"Well, there's a remedy for all things but death, which will be
sure to lay us flat one time or other."*
—Miguel de Cervantes

WHEN YOU PREVAIL in your case, the company must make
you whole. AIR21 remedies remind me of what you get when
you play a country western song backwards. You get your dog
back, your wife back, your life back. In this case you get your
job back, your pay back, but also *reasonable* attorney fees, lost
vacation, medical benefits, and such. Anything financial that you
lost because of the retaliatory action taken to make you whole is
fair game.

As previously stated, you only get "reasonable" attorney fees.
If your company wages a war of attrition on you, as Delta did with
me, that partial reimbursement may leave you with substantial
uncompensated costs.

When I settled with Delta for damages, after they lost
both the ruling and their appeal, we were simply heading to
court for reparations. After months of preparation and many
legal arguments Delta finally offered me "all" attorney fees and
what the judge ordered in the compensatory award. I settled. I
agreed to not state either number, but you can see the amount
awarded in the ruling regarding my compensatory damages in
the Decision and Order.[42] *The Seattle Times* article, *Petitt v. Delta*
is a great recap of this case.[43]

While the assumption is that the company made me whole, that was not the case.

There is no way anyone in litigation can win back seven years of their life after trial. You lose your health. Your spouse may lose their health. Family relationships break. You may even lose your life resulting from the stress, such as Captain Scott Patterson when American Airlines took him to battle. Are we ever made whole? No. But, for those who report safety this is not about money but about doing the right thing. And those unjustly persecuted in training or on the flight line, this is about saving your career.

The judge also has the power to order your company to post the ruling. Judge Morris ordered Delta to post my *Decision and Order* in every base and email to all employees. Delta argued and delayed that posting. When they finally posted it, they buried the document in hallways rarely wandered. They also falsely asserted they won in part in the embedded email link. We were filing a motion to remedy both those situations when they offered a settlement. On a side note, they also fought, and lost, to have CEO Ed Bastian's deposition removed from YouTube, and even requested an interlocutory review. Delta lost all arguments.

The humor in this fight over the posting and the video is that Delta's highly paid legal teams fighting the appeal forgot to ask the Administrative Review Board (ARB) to rule on the YouTube video removal and were remiss in objecting to the posting in the appeal. Most interesting in the appeal decision, the ARB identified Delta's failure to appeal the posting issue and even indicated that, had Delta objected to the posting order, it might have been rescinded. *Whoops.*

Regardless, we have now established case law for a judge to order the posting of your decision. While my decision no longer covers their backroom walls, Ed Bastian's YouTube video lives on, and the case was featured both on CNN and the front page of The Seattle Times.

Bastian's was the most laborious of all depositions because his lack of knowledge of the most basic things, that we assumed he knew, or should have known, killed the pace. Silence hangs in the video while Lee draws lines through irrelevant questions due to Bastian's ignorance, as Ed rolls his eyes, sighs, and places his head into his hand.

There is no point asking anyone the difference between a lake, an ocean, or a river, if the person stares at you with a blank look and tells you he doesn't know what water is. It's not his responsibility to know the elements of water, he's not a fish. In Bastian's case, he was the accountable executive of Delta's SMS program but lacked the requisite understanding of SMS. Ed Bastian's deposition video is on YouTube and appropriately titled, *Delta CEO Ed Bastian 1: I don't know what accountable executive means.*[44]

The fun begins about 25 minutes in when Bastian attempts to bullshit his way through SMS, then admits he doesn't know the components and that he has no personal involvement in the program. Yes, he was the accountable executive to the Delta SMS program. He was the captain of the airline and knew nothing about safety.

Bastian asserted his lack of knowledge was because he is not a pilot or flight operations leader. When told he was the accountable executive of the program, his face expressed sheer confusion as he stated, *"I don't know what accountable executive means."* Not a promising statement from the leader of an international airline. We thought this testimony would ensure Delta would settle. Yet, Delta still fought.

I also received vacation owed. Because I had followed the contract and battled the evaluation process when Delta attempted to buy off doctors, I got my job back and received backpay as a matter of the contract two years *before* we went to trial. I was working, back to flying, and able to finance my legal case because I was on full payroll for the remaining four and half years of litigation.

Judge Morris also identified damages to include loss of flight time, as flying is a perishable skill. I was subject to gossip, would never receive a management position, and would have the mental health issue on my FAA record for the rest of my career. If anything like this were to happen at a regional airline, I would argue this could damage my career by never achieving employment with a legacy carrier. Use this case precedent to support your claims.

Pain and suffering damages are difficult for a pilot to assert because you will never get damages that will cover your career, and if you claim severe mental anguish, you may well lose your medical. The airline legal team counts on this.

You will eventually write a list of all the damages, anything you can think of to include profit sharing, sick leave, vacation, etc., and attach the dollar amount. But first you must streamline your case in a document to communicate to your attorney. This document is something that you will use as your guide. What I'm about to tell you is what few attorneys advise, but it is priceless.

Chapter 14
Experience Teaches

"Life can only be understood backwards;
but it must be lived forwards."
—Soren Kierkegaard

AS I SAID, I am not an attorney, but I lived through the process and worked with the most knowledgeable and ethical AIR21 attorney who taught me this law. I have listened to legal advice from other firms and learned how to identify the good from the bad. Experiencing my legal process taught me a great deal. Experience is always the best teacher, and this is my gift to you.

Write a Timeline

THE ATTORNEY WHO wanted my case on contingency, if I dropped the safety concerns, asked me to write a timeline, so I did. While I opted to not drop the safety claim, I accepted the gift and power of a timeline. The maxim that preparation is the key to success is an understatement. Without it, you may go to great expense to learn that you might not even have a case. Not because the company did not retaliate, but because your case doesn't meet the law, and you did not explain the facts in sequence to your attorney.

Anyone going through retaliation knows the details are overwhelming. If you try to communicate all those details to your attorney, it will be difficult for him or her to track the case, identify the legality and the pertinent issues, and could cost you thousands of dollars trying to convey your story. I have listened to hours of these stories and worked hard to get the individuals to condense them into a paragraph to share with an attorney.

Before you ever see an attorney, *for any case*, you should write a succinct timeline. A timeline articulates the sequence of events and enables the attorney to see if you have a case based upon the dates, the action, the individuals involved and when the retaliation transpired. While I once listened to the stories of pilots, mechanics, and flight attendants for hours as they rambled, I now cut them off when they stray from the relevant issues. Still rarely do I get a direct answer. I make every effort to convey the importance of being succinct, sometimes to no avail.

I had spoken with a pilot for three hours, identified his protected activity, and provided advice on how to go forward and reminded him that he had only 90 days to file. He had thought they were discriminating against him because his captain said he could not understand him due to his accent. Shortly thereafter, they sent him on a flight with the "hatchet-man" a check airman reputed to focus on ways to fail a pilot on a check ride.

However, listening to the facts and digging to find out where this all started, I realized his accent was not the reason they wanted him gone. He wrote a safety report while on probation, which had surfaced during the FAA's investigation of the airline, not by the FAA, but by the company. The company then used the hatchet man as the tool to get rid of the pilot.

Sixty days later he called again. He had forgotten that I told him of the 90-day statute of limitation. During the previous sixty days a retired captain from another airline conducted an investigation on his behalf. This captain deduced that the pilot's termination was *unfair*, which didn't matter since the pilot was still on probation and not entitled to the protection of the just cause standard from the union. I tried to explain to the pilot that information gathered was great, but the opinion of this being unfair did not matter if he did not have a case.

Finally, over a period of multiple hours, and many calls, I explained how to articulate the facts that I believed to meet the AIR21 statute, so when he spoke to the attorney, he could articulate this in 10 minutes, and the attorney could tell him if he had a case.

What transpired was the pilot began speaking as I advised, and then the retired captain who investigated on his behalf, and had joined the call, stated in peremptory fashion: "This is not an AIR21 case."

The retired pilot then took over the discussion and ran down the path discussing who said what to whom, how the pilot felt, etc., and the unfairness of it all. Never did the pilot fully articulate to the attorney the nature of his protected activity and the retaliatory action taken against him. An hour and a half later they parted with nothing gained. This was an AIR21 case, not national origin discrimination. When I explained the facts to the attorney, he said, "have him write me a timeline with those facts."

I explained this to the pilot, and he said, "I tried to tell him (the attorney), but Captain… took over."

> **ADVICE**: Do not bring mom to your interview. If you bring anyone to an initial meeting with an attorney and they are not an attorney and take over, you state, "Sir, I appreciate your help, but you are not an attorney and I would like the AIR21 attorney to tell me if I have a case."

I advised this pilot to write the timeline with date, time, event, who was involved and their position. Five or six lines *only*. No details. Hours later he was still working on this. I reminded him of the brevity necessary. What he sent was a multi-page attachment. Without a retainer the attorney would not open and read the documents.

How to Write a Timeline:

Below is an example of what I would write today when looking for an attorney for my case. I omitted many of Delta's actions because, while they would be supporting material fact later, you must advise the attorney of the legally relevant facts first, and in the most efficient manner possible.

- January 28, 2016, Petitt provided a 54-page safety report regarding FAA violations, FAA approved training violations, and violations of pilot fatigue policy, etc., to Delta Senior VP of Flight Operations, Steve Dickson and VP of Flight Operations James Graham because she had a deep concern for public safety.
- February 16, 2016, Graham contacted Petitt and requested she meet with an HR safety investigator to investigate the report.
- March 7, 2016: Petitt met with HR safety investigator, Kelly Nabors. (Later learned she was the manager of the pass travel complaint department/EO) and they spoke for three hours on the content of Petitt's safety report, which Nabors held in her possession and wrote notes on.
- March 5, 2016: Petitt met with Chief Pilot Phil Davis, reporting concerns with crew rest, including Delta's failure to acknowledge deadhead as duty time per federal regulations.
- March 22, 2016: Phil Davis called Petitt into the Chief Pilot's office and provided a letter, dated March 17, 2016, grounding her from flight duty and ordering her to submit to compulsory mental health evaluation called a Section-15.
- Nobody at Delta would tell Petitt why they pulled her beyond stating, "It was something you said to Nabors."

From the above account, any attorney who knows the law will instantly identify the protected activity, communicated to senior management in good faith. The safety report was the reason for the meeting with Nabors therefore Nabors' damning account of

Petitt was related to Petitt's protected activity. In short, a prima facie case of retaliation was established shifting the burden of proof, by clear and convincing evidence, to Delta.

The fact that the March 5 report to the chief pilot regarding fatigue also occurred weeks before they pulled me could also have "contributed to" the grounding and compulsory psychiatric evaluation. The prima facie requirement of a nexus between the protected activity and the adverse action is supported by: (1) temporal proximity between the two, (2) the fact that Nabors' interrogation of me concerned my safety report, and (3) the company's refusal to adequately explain its decision to ground me.

During the process of discovery, I created a timeline on steroids to see the big picture of what Delta did, out of curiosity. I made a color-coded table with Date: Document number: To: From: Notes. This is something I referenced often, especially when we were deposing the bad guys. Even now, referring to the timeline to accurately discuss and articulate the facts is priceless.

I received documents from Dr. Altman that included hundreds of emails between him and Delta management, and I logged those in as DA (Dr. Altman) with the page number of his discovery in a date sequence. As Delta provided documents, I added those in red. However, Delta also withheld documents they asserted were "privileged" providing only the names of the correspondents and the date of the correspondence. I added those in blue identified as "privilege log."

For example, on 3/21/2015 PRIV-03 SVP of Communications Shinkle was communicating with CEO Bastian, SVP of legal Peter Carter, and SVP COO Gil West that was privileged. My notes copied Delta's statement: Privileged communication between client and counsel containing legal advice regarding Delta's response to Complainant's communications with Flight Operations.

I find it fascinating that they were discussing, "communications with flight operations" not "Pass travel/EO." The only people in Flight Operations were Dickson, Graham, and Davis.

These executives were discussing how they would proceed four days *after* Davis signed the letter, but one day *prior to* Davis providing me the letter to remove me from duty. This is a perfect example of what you can see when you get organized.

Davis had testified that he gave me the letter days *after* he signed it because it was important to do so in person. However, the truth was the CEO had not decided what to do yet. The CEO was talking with SVP of communications and the COO with an attorney present to keep it protected. They were deciding if they should remove me, and that discussion was the day before they acted upon it. That is a powerful connection.

I always found the Davis rationale based on the importance of in-person communication ridiculous because they emailed me on Christmas Eve that my career was over without anyone present. You will discover that there could be many thousands of documents and pages to review. Things get lost and forgotten because trial can extend for many years. From the point of Captain Graham deciding to send me to a psychiatric evaluation resulting from my requesting a meeting, to the settlement over damages, seven years had lapsed.

While Delta pulled me at the end of March 2016, my timeline began in November of 2015, because discovery identified that they had already planned to send me to an evaluation and were orchestrating a pretext. That, too, is telling. As a matter of law, Judge Morris also identified those November 2015 communications as protected activity in his *Decision and Order*:

> *"The parties agree that Complainant's submittal of her safety report to Respondent was a protected activity, and the Tribunal additionally finds the November 3, 2015, email constituted protected activity.* [45]

Begin small to first outline your case for an attorney. Then, after you know you have a case, go to work and allow it to grow. I subsequently found all sorts of nuggets within my 86-page timeline.[46]

If It Feels Wrong, It Is!

MULTIPLE ATTORNEYS SAID I had to wait until I lost my job. ALPA tried to convince me to use the grievance process that could take years. My ALPA attorney told me to avoid the neuropsychological testing and instead take an unpaid leave of absence, in which case I would never have returned to Delta.

Delta, ALPA representatives, and AMAS tried to convince me to **not** get my medical certificate. ALPA even told me if I did choose to get a medical, to not disclose that I was seeing a psychiatrist on the 8500 document, because the examination was company ordered. Logic would dictate that a company ordered psych evaluation might be of concern to the FAA. I did not listen.

Delta and ALPA attempted to convince me to go on disability to get my ALPA insurance that I had paid into, but I would have had to say I was bipolar. I am not omniscient, but when something feels wrong, it probably is. Logic told me that if I signed a legal document stating I agreed with the diagnosis, that assertion might diminish my argument that I did not have one. Yet, I know many pilots who have fallen into this trap for money. It has never served them well long term. Short term gains that lead to long term losses are never a good thing.

Furthermore, if had I waited until termination, after the bipolar diagnosis, to file a complaint, I believe I would have lost. If I had not claimed retaliation for placing me into the Section 15 and *waited* until the diagnosis, nine-months *after* they removed me from duty, I would have had no claim due to the statute of limitations on what started this event. Delta could also *legally* remove me from duty because of the bipolar diagnosis. My AIR21 case would have been dealt a fatal blow because Delta would claim they were only listening to the doctors and had no choice but to let me go.

If Delta purchased the tie-breaking neutral examiner, as they tried, with two of three doctors then confirming the same diagnosis, I would have lost my medical and been totally reliant upon the AIR21 statute to return to work. Yet, if I had not filed it,

I would have nothing to rely on. Then I would have been fighting a legal case without income.

I would have no case against the doctors for malpractice because they work for the airline and were not my doctor. If two out of three doctors said I had a problem, and then I claimed, "but they put me into this Section 15 of which I did not belong," Delta would claim that event happened 9 months earlier, and my statute of limitations was only 3 months. You must assert retaliation at the first indication of when they take action against you.

Furthermore, had I not followed the Section 15 process, and not taken the neuropsychological tests, but instead taken an unpaid leave of absence, as directed by ALPA, I never would never have returned because I cannot undo that option. In addition, had I listened to ALPA and not disclosed I was seeing a company-ordered psychiatrist on my medical, I could have lost my medical certificate for falsification of records.

The fact that I retained my first-class medical certificate, indicated that the FAA determined I was fine the entire time during the evaluation. If faced with a company-ordered retaliatory mental health challenge, retain your medical and do not allow it to lapse. Do not allow your union to suck you into a time delay with the grievance process. When the company wants an employee gone, the union today will frequently not protect you.

Contrary to the history of airline unionism, which traditionally defended the job security of its members as a paramount objective, this appears to no longer be the case. I say that with a caveat, because I know AMFA supports their mechanics. *All* their mechanics. Because if you are part of the union, you are in the club. As it should be with any union. However, pilot unions are no longer such an animal. Union officers no longer volunteer for their positions out of the goodness of their hearts to help those in need. Today these appointments are profit driven, and a pilot, as a union officer, can make far more money while working less flight hours. If the company wants you gone, then you can expect a level of injustice with your union.

I do know union representatives who volunteer for the right reason. But it's impossible to be in that club and retain your ethical convictions. The most common statement is, "If I take a stand I will be removed, and I can't do anything if I'm not in position." This is a hamster on a wheel that goes nowhere. With that said, there are some fabulous representatives that are going out of their way for pilots under challenging circumstances. One such representative has even paid for legal advice outside the union to help those pilots she represents and today the union is working to remove her from her position for going that extra mile. I would love to name the select few representatives who are fighting for you beyond the good old boys' club of ALPA, but they would be gone overnight if I did.

Another pilot contacted me for help and explained her Chinese heritage and, as new hire at a major airline, her award on the B777. But due to political issues in China the passport moved to extended delay status. Initially the union worked to transfer the pilot to the B737 until the passport arrived. Unfortunately, the pilot told management the reason why the delayed passport and the airline decided to terminate this pilot asserting she could not fly all routes.

The law required the airline to accommodate this pilot, if the passport delay issue was national origin related and would not cause harm to the airline by doing so. The ALPA representatives told the pilot that reinstatement would occur once the passport was in hand, and not to worry about the termination.

ALPA does not have the power to reinstate the pilot unilaterally. Nothing was in writing. And ALPA does not legally represent a pilot on probation. ALPA legal should have advised this pilot that an EEOC charge could provide legal leverage to support retention to the position, as going to the B737 was a reasonable accommodation. Instead, they led the pilot to believe they were working on the pilot's behalf. This pilot exceeded the applicable statute of limitations.

If you are facing job action, thank the union for their help, but take matters in your own hands as well. If the union is on the up and up, then you will be working as a team. If not, you may just save your career. At the end of the day, the union will not defend you if the company wants you gone.

Facts Not Feelings

YOUR ATTORNEY IS not your therapist. When you write your timeline or speak to an attorney do not tell him or her how they made you feel, just state the facts. As far as that goes, never tell the judge what to think, just give him the facts so he will come to the same conclusion that you have. If you present the facts, not feelings, the judge will see the connection. You can express your feelings when it comes to damages.

Maintain Your Composure

WHEN YOU'RE IN court, the judge is watching *you*. Impressions of your stability will either support or contradict the company's assertions. At the end of my trial Judge Morris said:

> *I want to note for the record I paid close attention during these nine days; particularly, I want to talk about the demeanor of the Complainant. My observation is that—my impression was that she was alert, bright, engaging, confident, in some cases one could even perceive as being cocky. However, I, at no time, saw any type of emotion that would indicate anything consistent with what Ms. Nabors observed. Now, I want to state that specifically for the record, because this is one point that bothers me in this case. Everything I've seen in this file, with the exception of Ms. Nabors' report is not what was being reported by Ms. Nabors. I don't know how to resolve that, but it is diametrically opposed to everything I've heard from witnesses and my observations of the Complainant during these proceedings.[47]*

Most companies claim behavioral problems when attempting to rid itself of a pilot, and then they push until you break to prove their point. The irony of the judge's statement was it came during the final day of trial during which I felt the most angst because Captain Phil Davis was smiling directly at me from the stand as he attempted to justify the company's retaliation. More than torment, I was pissed.

His misrepresentations were not harming me in the eyes of the judge, but he was distorting the truth in an effort to make himself look good by telling the judge he agreed with me. But he made assertions that were not true about my concern for pilots commuting. My only concern was the company's method of putting pilots on positive space with a green slip, a double paid trip, not calling it duty time and therefore *not* paying them for the travel or providing them any crew rest. Not to mention, the entire legal process had been exhausting. Trial started in March, and it was already May. While I did not fall apart on this final day, I did find myself holding my breath when the judge asked Captain Davis if he ever saw me cry, and he paused.

I was thinking *don't you dare lie about that*! We all waited for his answer. The courtroom silent as the guillotine was about to fall upon my neck. Or would it?

He finally said, "No. I've never seen her cry." To date, I'm unsure if he answered that question truthfully because of the potential challenge as to why he didn't say something earlier, or because his legal team did not tell him how to reply, or because when I found him sitting alone in the court early that day, having missed his opportunity to be escorted to lunch, I gave him half my sandwich. These are the mysteries of life and perplexities of human nature that we may never understand.

Don't underestimate the power of kindness even to those who are misguided souls. Yet, the moral of this story is to maintain your composure. The judge is watching.

Follow Your Contract

THE BEST ADVICE I ever got was to follow the contract. This was Lee Seham's advice. If your contract says you jump through a hoop, do it. Just because the company broke the law, does not mean you get to break your contract. Many people told me not go to Delta's psychiatrist, that I would lose my medical. Initially I did not believe that to be the case, until I met Dr. Altman who asked me if I had expressed my milk to feed my children 30 years earlier. At that time, I realized this was not a legitimate evaluation.

Did it matter he was a paid hitman? No. The company may pay someone to off you, but you do not have control over that. You only have control of your actions. If the contract says you go, you go. Sort the garbage later. Do what you are supposed to do, and then fight their wrongs.

Get the FAA involved and Retain Your Medical.

THE REASON THAT your employee contract dictates that the company will *not* advise the FAA they pulled you for a mental health evaluation until the medical review process is complete is *not* to protect you, but to ensure they get their way when paying a doctor to misdiagnose you. Once the FAA pulls your medical certificate, you're done. Not that you cannot get it back, but the effort and odds are not in your favor, and it could take many years. In my case I retained my medical because I applied for it. Delta was not pleased by my actions.

My AME, Aviation Medical Examiner, knew what was happening, and after discussion we simply noted on the medical application (8500 document), that all my psychiatrist visits were a result of a, *"Political corporate action."* One of two things happened. 1) The FAA fully understood what was ongoing, or 2) the FAA never looks at the records of any medical that the AME does not defer.

I suspect the latter, because they don't have the time to read records for thousands of pilots if the AME doesn't question your certificate. Either way, the FAA issued my medical. Delta challenged it and called Dr. Michael Berry, the FAA Deputy Federal Flight Surgeon at the time, to have it revoked. Until then, my ability to hold a first class medical never came into question.

There was only one snag when my AME became fearful to issue my medical after Dr. Altman's diagnosis, despite the Mayo Clinic aviation department writing to him that I was not bipolar and qualified for a first class medical with a report attached. The Mayo clinic team consisted of thirteen doctors and one a bipolar specialist. Despite this assessment, my AME became fearful because FAA representative Warren Silberman, a friend of his, warned him that he should no longer support me. Warren even referred to Delta as "the baddies" and this was a political timebomb and he did not want my AME backed into a corner.

My AME wanted to defer my medical license. I told him if he did that, I may never get it back. While afraid to get involved in the politics and risk his license by giving me my medical, he queried the FAA regional flight surgeon, Dr. Brett Wyrick, to ask for his help. Wyrick had no qualms with issuing me my first class medical.

Delta, livid, then reached out to the Deputy Federal Flight Surgeon, Dr. Berry to revoke my medical. Dr. Berry told Dr. Wyrick to investigate further and read Dr. Altman's full report and make another determination. Wyrick read all documents associated with my case and came to the same conclusion—I deserved a first class medical.

Had I not been issued my medical, I would have not returned to work to finance this legal battle. If Delta had not opened this up to the FAA, then even the tie-breaking neutral psychiatrist may have supported his "esteemed colleague." Yes, my neutral doctor knew Dr. Altman, but this issue was now on a different playing field with the FAA involved and obtaining their support.

After the medical appeals board certified me as fine, it would be difficult for the neutral doctor go against the FAA. Especially if he was just entering the business to certify pilots and wanted to do these evaluations on behalf of the FAA. So, Delta undermined its own plan by contacting the FAA. On a side note, the third doctor, in my opinion, is an honest man because he disclosed to me that Delta offered to pay for and fly out anyone to assist his evaluation, and they stated, "No expense spared."

Logically speaking, if the Mayo Clinic bipolar specialist said I was fine, along with 12 other specialists, why would Delta be forcing this issue? They would not. Pay attention to the logic and stupidity of what the other side claims. If you can see it, let the judge see it too.

Do not fear pursuing your medical when there is a political corporate action against you. The real strength comes from an AME who will overcome his fear, and do the right thing, because he knows the truth. Your AME will determine what happens next. Don't ever allow them to convince you that deferring your medical is something you should accept and will benefit you. I told my AME that I would never get my medical back if he deferred it. That was the very reason he reached out to Dr. Wyrick. Wyrick had no problem doing the right thing.

Of note, Dr. Michael Berry had worked for Delta as their in-house doctor back in the day when a pilot pension was still a thing. A pilot identified pension fraud and Delta decided to remove him with a mental health claim and Dr. Berry was the go-to doctor. Delta lost the case, and a judge ordered that Dr. Berry could never work for Delta again. Dr. Berry left Delta and went directly to the FAA, and eventually became the FAA Deputy Flight Surgeon. If your mouth dropped open wondering how the hell that is possible, you're not alone.

Judge Morris was deeply concerned when he learned that an FAA doctor, the Deputy Federal Flight Surgeon, had worked for Delta and knew that Delta was keeping pilots' mental health concerns secret from the FAA. After the conclusion of my trial, Dr. Michael Berry subsequently retired.

Plan for Your Return

TWO ATTORNEYS TOLD me that I did not have a legal case until termination. However, one of them told me the company would do one of two things: 1) pay a doctor to say I was medically unfit, or 2) keep me out as long as possible and provide minimum simulator training and fail me.

I had no control over Delta paying a doctor, but I did have control over my required training. Therefore, while I was out, on payroll, going through the motions of the first evaluation, I bid a different aircraft for my return, on the B777. When I returned, I would get a full training program, not minimum training. Do what you can, the rest you figure out as it comes along.

If you are in a holding pattern waiting to return to work, you better be studying your airplane daily as you can expect the most difficult check ride of your life upon your return.

Delta did pay a doctor, and they kept me out for two years without flying and then put a hit on me in the simulator. Thanks to an ethical retired instructor, working in a contractor status, my efforts, a full training program, and a sim partner that was a witness, the Delta strategy of an attack in training, upon my return, did not work. I earned my B777 type-rating, having not flown for two years.

Disability

WHEN THEY CALL you crazy do not take disability stating you have a problem. I know a pilot who did this, and she never returned. You should not accept money for a disability you do not have, and you cannot win a case stating you are not bipolar if you are accepting payments because of a bipolar diagnosis. The union, the company, and your rapidly emptying pocketbook will try to convince you otherwise, but don't do it.

I had insurance with ALPA that I paid into that should have provided me a year of half-pay for circumstances like this, yet they *refused to* pay me because I refused to sign the document stating I was bipolar. I still believe forsaking that money was well worth it. There are things more valuable than money in our world. We die with integrity; the money is left behind.

Depositions

YOU WILL DEPOSE witnesses to obtain their testimony under oath. However, only what ends up in court is allowed in your final brief.

For example, if you depose a Chief Pilot who says he was setting you up, you must ask that question in court to use that statement in your final summary. Trying to be sneaky and ask questions to "catch" the witness in a lie during the deposition is a waste of time. You simply ask fact-based questions that build your case. Those statements should be asked and answered, again, in court. If they change their testimony, well, that might not look so good to the judge, and the company's resort to shifting rationales will support your case.

In my case, James Graham testified in a deposition, under oath, on December 18th telling one story. In trial he told a completely different story when Delta's attorney questioned him. Lee wrote like crazy during this testimony, while I sat with a crease between my eyebrows wondering where the hell this new narrative came from. Then during the cross-examination, Lee addressed this altered testimony in the following manner:

Seham: Now, sir, you were deposed on December 18th, 2018, in this matter, correct?

Graham: Correct.

Sehasm: And you took an oath to tell the truth, correct?

Graham: Correct.

Seham: And you were advised, at the time, that the transcript might be used in Court?

Graham: Yes.

Seham: And you were represented by Mr. Ira Rosenstein, at that deposition, correct?

Graham: Correct.

Seham: If I could direct your attention to page 28 of this deposition.[48]

Page 28 was completely opposite to anything Graham had said on the stand. Lee continued to challenge his trial testimony that contradicted everything he had testified in his deposition, by referring to his deposition over and over again. Rosenstein, Delta's attorney, challenged the use of the deposition in such a manner, and the judge overruled him. I was thinking, *Isn't that the purpose of a deposition?*

Graham's disposition went from upright, confident, and assertive, to slouching and red-faced, with sideways glares at his legal team. I was unable to ascertain if his look was *what the hell did you get me into?* or *get me off this stand now!* Graham's trial testimony deviated so markedly from his deposition testimony, that Lee spontaneously asked, "*Have you had any illness between the time of the deposition and today?*"

I almost spewed my water.

Graham said, "No."

This time Graham directed his venomous glare at me.

Videotape Your Depositions

I HAD NOT realized how powerful video is. The written word does not convey the full picture. If your witness pauses for a few minutes formulating a response, transcripts do not show that delay. The transcript reads as if this were a rapid response. A video depicts shifting eyes, glares, and erratic behavior, all of which do not show in a transcript.

During a deposition with Lincoln Bisbee, another Delta attorney, Bisbee and Lee engaged in a heated debate that began with Lee asking him to not yell, followed by Bisbee yelling, "I'm not yelling!"

I exchanged a glance with the court reporter who smiled. If I were the court reporter I would have written, "yes he is" in the transcript. Regardless, a video would show this behavior. And this was the very reason we videotaped Graham's testimony, because of Bisbee's behavior. You can see all sorts of emotions with that one.

Graham's deposition is on YouTube. Search *Delta SVP James Graham 1, Delta SVP James Graham 2…* on up through 6. I only wished we had a video of Dr. Faulkner, Delta's in house doctor, whose behavior was erratic in his Tommy Bahama shirt in the middle of winter. He blew a fuse when we asked him if he was on his self-disclosed anti-depressants when he evaluated me, and even more so when asked if the Hippocratic Oath applied to the Section 15 process. He finally admitted without the Hippocratic Oath document in front of him, he could not answer the question.

Discovery

ALL PARTIES MUST provide responses to interrogatories, document requests, and requests for admissions. Interrogatories are a written set of questions from one party in a case by another party which must be answered under oath. Requests for admissions are statements that you request the other party to admit or deny. The intent of this process is to build a body of undisputed facts for the court. If both parties can agree upon the facts this reduces court time.

A document request is a demand for the production of relevant documents, and you can demand documents of all types. Request all emails and written communications to and from each person that could be involved in your case, as well as documents that could prove your case regarding policy, and procedures, etc. None of this is what it seems. If your company is like Delta, they will not admit to anything until the final hour, if ever.

Your company may not even follow the court order. In my case, Delta did not give us thousands of pages of documents. We know this to be true because we got them from Dr. Altman, and they originated from Delta. While this is against the law, I opted to not go after Delta because it would have cost time and money, and we already got them from Dr. Altman. We could spend money, fight, win, and get nothing for it.

In your case you should also request documents from a third party if applicable. Think about who else was involved in your case that might have knowledge. If this is airline related, the FAA may know something, and you can do a Freedom of Information Act (FOIA) request.[49]

You are probably wondering why Dr. Altman provided us all the dirt on Delta. Lee had sent Dr. Altman an ESI—Notice of Need and Demand to Preserve Electronically stored Information. This is a scary letter of warning designed to prevent the recipient from subsequently claiming that he lost or inadvertently destroyed the information at a later date because he was ordered to protect it. Dr. Altman gave us everything based on the ESI.[50]

Dr. Altman may have thought Delta would provide this information, so perhaps he believed non-compliance would not look good for him. Perhaps his ego was such he believed he was invincible, or his attorney advised him accordingly, or that he had nothing to lose because Delta was protecting him. He gave us the incriminating details of how they did what they did and why. At the end of the day, he forfeited his medical license.

Dr. Altman's license forfeiture is another story. It took me over three years of persuasion with the Illinois medical board for them to finally take action against him. My final and convincing argument was that it would not look good for their agency if a pilot had an actual mental health problem with nothing to live for, and Dr. Altman sent him back into the sky for money, because the pilot was the highest bidder. I explained the Germanwings fatal crash, where the pilot intentionally crashed the plane. This discussion brought immediate action after three years of delay.

Two of the *many* complaints against Dr. Altman were Delta pilots, mine and Captain Protack's. As it turned out, each complaint against Dr. Altman had to stand alone, as the Illinois medical board does not combine all the complaints against a doctor. Therefore, ten complaints require ten different investigations.

Vladmir Lozovskiy, the prosecuting attorney told me that Altman planned to fight both the Delta cases in court. The others were not strong enough to stand alone. I waited for Vladmir to advise me of trial dates, and was looking forward attending both trials.

When I learned many months later that they had combined our cases, settled out of court, and Dr. Altman forfeited his medical license I was surprised. Vladmir had not notified me, and when I reached out to find out what transpired he refused to discuss the case. There were shenanigans on going.

Our cases had two different case numbers. However, a FOIA request on my case returned a few pages, and it was based upon Protack's case. *What the hell?* My file against Dr. Altman *disappeared* in the offices of the Illinois medical department and the prosecuting attorney's office. Mine was no small file, as I had provided over 700 pages to the medical board regarding my case. All was gone.

The reality of this Illinois investigation is that a trial with Protack would have been of no issue for Delta. Dr. Altman simply wrote a letter of extortion to Protack advising him if he filed charges or contacted an attorney, he would be unfit for duty, but if he returned to the evaluation, he might be fine. No evidence beyond that letter had surfaced. This was all on Altman, and nothing on Delta, despite we know who paid him. My case, however, would open a can of worms for Delta. They did not want mine to go to court, because their actions, payment, and communications would become a media nightmare again. Delta needed this settled more than Dr. Altman did.

These are the facts. You get to decide what happened to the missing files and Dr. Altman's forfeiting his license without a trial. However, this is not the first time files would disappear.

Delta's federal violations, which occurred while Steve Dickson was Senior VP of Flight Operations, disappeared from the FAA records while Steve Dickson was the acting FAA administrator. FAA investigator, David Smith, advised me as much and told me this had never happened before, and he had no idea where they went.

I suppose, hypothetically, that there is no better way to sanitize your airline's records than by placing the guy who was ultimately responsible for the violations into the very office that has access to those records and ability to dispose thereof. To say

I was highly involved in tracking the behavior of these guys is an understatement.

Be Involved in Your Case

BECOME INVOLVED IN your case. You are not the *passenger* of your life and should never go passively for the ride especially in a legal battle. You know company policies, rules, and events. Your attorney knows the law. As previously mentioned, my initial attorney filed my complaint and did not allow me to read it first. He only provided it *after* he filed. He had named American Airlines not Delta. We refiled. But he could have easily misunderstood facts as well. When Delta filed a response, they cited the Northwest case that my attorney was unaware and never reviewed to see if it were true.

As I worked with Lee, he always sent me a draft of everything he wrote to review and edit. I read and track-changed for content. This began our process of working together. Lee would not file *anything* unless I had the chance to read it for accuracy. He is a wordsmith with the facts and the law, but no attorney can fully understand our airline world or remember all our policies and procedures when dealing with so many different airlines, or the details of federal regulations that continually change.

When I heard that a flight attendant lost during the motion to dismiss phase I was heartbroken because she could have prevailed. As it turned out, the attorneys did not include all the facts in her complaint, and the reason for that loss. The facts they had unintentionally omitted may have enabled her to continue, but her case ended before it began.

Being engaged is powerful for many reasons. Not only does it ensure factual accuracy, enabling an in-depth understanding of the law, but it helps you to mentally take action instead of a being a victim. Most importantly, be honest and convey everything to your attorney. If you have something you did that might not look good when uncovered, tell your attorney. It's better to be prepared and address the issue head on. Besides, it might not be that bad after all and could provide an example to your decision-making, judgement, and risk mitigation.

A pilot and his attorney called to discuss my case as they were preparing for trial. He disclosed a situation and told me he was nervous because technically he broke a regulation on a flight. I listened to the event and knew that I would have done the exact same thing.

He had received an aircraft swap on the third flight of a three-leg day and the autopilot was inoperative. The logbook write-ups however said that functionality was intermittent. Maintenance could not duplicate it on the ground. Therefore, they dispatched without the use of the autopilot. But this had been a long day, with an unexpected aircraft swap and they decided to see if it worked. It did, and they used it.

I smiled listening to this story. I suggested that his attorney bring this up on his examination and control the narrative, and told them both what I would say in front of a judge who was a pilot and understood safety and the law.

Question: *"Have you ever flown a plane in violation of a federal regulation?"*

Response: *"Yes."*

Question: *"Can you please explain?"*

Response: *"We had a last-minute aircraft swap, which found us scrambling to get to the new plane and preflight it, thus our adrenaline was high. But after departure, as we droned through the night, adrenaline depleted, we realized our level of fatigue could be an issue. The logbook indicated the autopilot was intermittent, so using my captain authority to deviate regulations in the interest of safety, I decided to try it. It worked. I maintained a constant vigilance, but this enabled us to expand our situational awareness and improved the safety of our flight."*

Question: *"If you could do that flight over, would you do it again?"*

> **Response:** *"Absolutely not. With what I learned about the potential for fatigue after an adrenaline rush, I would have cancelled this last flight without an autopilot."*

After I spoke these words, he told me that was *exactly* why he did it. And he would never do that again.

Don't hide behind your mistakes but use them to show your decision making and the lessons learned in the process, and how you would proceed next time. That concept is the essence of ASAP, and why employees can self-disclose without issue. And if no discipline occurred for the error you made, then the company acknowledges what transpired did not warrant action.

Honesty

I HAD SPENT dozens of hours over many months trying to help a pilot who at the end of the day decided his whistleblower attorney, on contingency, was his saving grace. This pilot was the reason I decided to author this book. In hindsight, I could have written it in the hours I gave him, to no avail.

I also wondered if his law firm had done an AIR21 before. The reason being the pilot did not have a case because he had not received an adverse action. He went out sick before the company retaliated for anything. He was rapidly losing temporal proximity to the *only* event that could provide him a case, but he would have to return to work to see if the company would retaliate. But he refused to return despite my efforts to explain why he should.

This pilot was out on sick leave, which extended into disability, and he was simply fearful to go back because ALPA hearsay told him that if he returned, the company would see he never flew a Delta plane again. To make that statement an adverse action, he needed ALPA to put in writing which company official said that if he returned, he would be terminated. And even then, it would be subjective. As now, it was just gossip. I told him ALPA would say, *"I didn't take notes, and I do not recall that conversation."* And that's exactly what they stated.

The legal team sent a demand letter, and he sat at home thinking Delta would buy him off. My advice was to study and go back to work and pass training. He listened to his attorneys. Apparently, their demand letter did not work, as he sent me a copy of his complaint that they had filed, and all sorts of problems jumped off the page, including a false statement that he had submitted a declaration to OSHA, for my case, which was not true.

Do NOT write false statements.

My frustration and disappointment at the dozens of false statements that Delta's attorneys wrote in briefs and asserted during trial was at an all-time high. That's not actually true. I wanted to smack the bastards. They lied and lied again.

But just because *they* lie, you do not have to. Be honest as it will establish your credibility. And if you're not honest, the judge will be skeptical of anything honest you may say. The Complainant can't lie, but when the company defends itself, anything goes. The only reason they are defending themselves is because they lied as to why they took action against you.

You must be honest. Tell the truth. Besides, it's the easiest thing to remember.

Those Zealous Advocates

I LEARNED THAT Delta attorneys cited cases that either had no relevance at all, or they wrote false assertions. Why would they misrepresent these cases if they were easily verifiable? Because nobody checks. The judge will not look up and review the case law. And if your attorney lacks knowledge of the case and doesn't take the time to review it, then these false statements prevail.

I realized early in my case that Delta's legal team could write false claims regarding case law. After Lee identified that Northwest case, I began reviewing all Delta's cited cases.

Every motion and document that Delta's legal team, Morgan Lewis and Bockius, cited, I asked Lee to send me the case brief. In my opinion, in most cases they either flat out falsified the document regarding the case, or they interpreted it in such a manner that one might think they were incompetent in their ability to read and synthesize data. Or they were intentionally misrepresenting the facts. When your company has no case, they will manufacture something. Count on it.

I recently heard of a case in London that an attorney had used AI to write a legal brief that incorrectly cited cases and the judge noticed. Therefore, I Googled to find the information for this book. However, during my search I discovered a New York lawyer faced charges in 2023, because a judge found the references to cases he cited didn't exist. The lawyer had used AI and did not know that the content was false.[51]

I'm uncertain if Delta's attorneys used AI, or simply fabricated their arguments out of whole cloth, but either way reviewing case law is a powerful way to find information that will support *your* case. Look up those cases and you will learn that they may benefit you. And in those cases, there are also citations for other cases that could be equally supportive.

End of Trial

TRIAL IS OVER and now you will write a 60-page brief. In my case, the judge only allowed 50 pages substantive and allocated the remaining ten pages to damages. The judge will give you a date the brief is due. The brief must have a one-inch margin, double spaced 12-point Times New Roman font. Footnotes can be 11-point Times New Roman. The company will respond with their 60-page brief, and only 50 pages substantive. Because I was the plaintiff and had the initial burden of proof, I was able to respond to Delta's brief, but I only had 25 pages for that response.

This is the law. You write a brief, the Respondent writes a brief, and then you reply, and the judge will rule on those documents. This is the very reason you need an attorney who has knowledge and can concisely place all facts in an articulate manner before the judge in minimal pages. Every word counts.

On a funny note, Delta's attorney, Ira Rosenstein, with Morgan Lewis and Bockius, does not like this rule as identified by the following exchange.

Rosenstein: I have a question on the briefing. You said that you were going to give the Complainant a reply brief, because they had the burden, if I understood?
Judge Morris: Yes.
Rosenstein: Their burden is only on the first prong, correct?
Judge Morris: Right.
Rosenstein: So, is there an opportunity either for Respondent to have a reply on the part of the case for which Respondent has the burden on the second one?
Judge Morris: No.
Rosenstein: That doesn't seem fair and I'll state that for the record.
Judge Morris: It's noted, preserved for appeal.
Rosenstein: You can count on it.
Judge Morris: It's your prerogative. Anything else?
(No verbal response.)
Judge Morris: All right. This hearing is closed.[52]

"It's not fair!"

No, IT'S NOT. But primarily it's not fair for the employee who must spend money to defend themselves and fight for their career when an airline is the bad actor. Life is not fair, but you can survive and succeed if you know the law and use it to your advantage. I did.

What you have on your side, is that the highly paid law firm representing the company may not have the knowledge that you do after reading this book. I don't think Delta's in-house attorney's do either. Will they read this? Perhaps because Ed's, Graham's, and Steve's photos are on the cover. Can they stop you from applying the principles? No. We can only hope this might be a deterrent if they know you are prepared.

Writing Your Brief After Trial

YOU CAN ONLY include in your brief what you or the other side presented in trial. I state that with a caveat as you can cite legal cases.

In Delta's closing response, they highly emphasized, overly so, the Germanwings accident. They said they had to send me to a psychiatric evaluation out of an abundance of caution. They reimbursed me, I got my job back, and there was no harm no foul. I laid awake the night after reading their assertions, thinking about the statement that they *had to* send me to a mental health evaluation because of the Germanwings pilot, and their claim that I experienced no harm. Everything about this high-stress event was damaging to my health.

The judge knew there was no comparing me to the Germanwings pilot. He also knew that there was in fact harm. But this is only because he witnessed firsthand the testimony of all players in our 9-day trial, as he had even assessed me. But would the administrative review board (ARB), who would be ruling on the appeal, make the same assessment if *all* they had to go on were 50 pages, and Delta's argument they were doing this out of a preponderance of caution? I wasn't so sure.

Lee and I discussed this concern, and I told him there were lawsuits against the Germanwings airline from US passengers. Bingo! Lee found case law. Case law *is* allowed to be admitted in the final brief, even if it was not previously used in trial. What Lee discovered was the Germanwings pilot's history.

We compared a mentally challenged pilot who was in and out psychiatric hospitals and failed multiple training events, to me, a pilot working on a PhD with no training failures, multiple degrees, and no mental health issues. This comparison in one paragraph, quashed Delta's only argument left to subjective analysis. Anyone reading this who was not involved in the case could easily identify the ridiculousness of their assertion. Find the case law that supports you and use it.

Mindset

HAVE FAITH THAT you will prevail, and do not allow the negative "what ifs" to enter your mind. Sometimes it's harder than you think, but it doesn't have to be.

After my mom had read Dr. Altman's report she said, "This is *really* bad. You'll never get back."

I snapped, "Yes, I will! This report has no foundation of anything medical and is a load of crap."

I am certain there are other people, like my mother, who believe simply because a man, who is a doctor, tells you something it must be true. But don't you believe it. I had a choice to go into whiny pity me mode and agree with her that I would never get back, or to call it bullshit and fight. I chose to fight the ridiculousness of it all.

Thankfully, months later Dr. Steinkraus at the Mayo Clinic said, "We all read it," meaning the 10 doctors involved my case read his report, and "we can see a political corporate action versus a medical diagnosis." Prior to that, Forensic Psychologist, Stewart Gitlow, gave me the specifics as to the medically false assertions.

I took the Altman 366-page report and wrote a rebuttal with facts, using Gitlow's language for the medical terms. Within that Altman report was another version, of many, of Nabors's reports and I wrote a rebuttal to that too. I never believed they would get away with this. There were teary-eyed moments, lost sleep, and I had to suck a deep breath or two, unbelieving the length of deception that both Delta and their attorneys lowered themselves to, but then I dug in with renewed resolve.

You must always believe you will survive. A pilot never stops flying their plane, and nobody should ever give up fighting for their life or their career that they worked so hard to achieve. The truth is, they might win. But thinking that, as you struggle day to day, is unproductive and will not serve you well.

During my psychiatric interview Dr. Altman said, "You must have been really worried about that." I suspected that statement was to support my alleged paranoia. But when I told him I did not worry because that was a waste of time, he became argumentative. I tried to explain that if I had a concern, I took action. Worry served nobody well. This became an issue with him and a point of contention at trial, because of my particularity for certain words. He testified that he used the word incorrectly between worry and concern. But that was not the discussion. The guy was an educated nut job, and he didn't understand. I hope you do.

Do what you can to solve the problem, and at the end of the day whatever happens will. Do not worry or think about the worst case while you're in the fight. Do not ruin your life further by worrying about something that may not happen. All you are doing is putting negative energy into the world. The worst may happen, but if you are doing all you can to prevent that then the worry won't help.

NDA

IF YOUR COMPANY asks for an NDA when they offer a settlement, you do not have to say yes. Your company may assert this is a condition of the settlement; but think of this logically.

1. They want a settlement only because they know you'll win.
2. They don't want their behavior known to others.

If you go to court, not only could this become a media nightmare for them, as mine did, but they have already acknowledged that you have a case and the reason they want to settle. Why allow them to win on all accounts?

Settlement is the smartest move, but not at the sacrifice of others coming behind you. I refused to sign an NDA but agreed to not tell the world what Delta paid in attorney fees and not state what they paid me. But it was okay for me to state I got the dollar amount the judge awarded, just not say the number. I let the media spread the second dollar figure as it was in the decision and order. Settlement numbers do not matter, but the events to prevent this from happening again do. Don't allow them to silence you.

Because I did not sign an NDA, I can speak openly about this case to help others, author this book, and write a memoir. The only way to improve safety and world integrity is to be free to speak about safety lapses and call out every pilot who participated in this action and took money and/or promotion to allow Delta management to do what they did against me.

Why would I take money to allow Delta to do this to others? I would be no better than those who harmed me.

Do not sign an NDA. Every person I have spoken to who had signed an NDA has regretted that decision. There might be people out there who are happy and whole and don't want to talk about what happened to them and feel that the after-tax settlement was worth it, but I have yet to meet even one person. The settlement will haunt you, as it does me, but I can speak of the illegal actions without fear of further retaliation and continue to fight for others.

Delta engaged in a war of attrition against me that lasted seven years and they finally asked me to settle on *damages* out of court. I did, but I refused to sign an NDA. They agreed to accept a confidentiality provision limited to the dollar value of the settlement. Therefore, I am free to speak to you about my case and how you might learn from it. One day you may also want to author a book or an article about your experience.

Chapter 15
Lessons Learned

"Life is a succession of lessons which must be lived to be understood. All is riddle, and the key to a riddle is another riddle."
—*Ralph Waldo Emerson*

Things I Learned to be True

1. Depending on the state, you may not be able to sue a doctor for malpractice if he is engaged by the airline to evaluate you as a third party. There is no physician-patient relationship.
2. If that doctor, paid by the company, prescribes any medication, directs you to see a psychiatrist, requests bloodwork, etc., he may have established a physician-patient relationship. At that point, you could file for malpractice.
3. Doctors have malpractice insurance, and if you have facts to win, you can engage in settlement yourself with the insurance company.
4. You can only win fraud if "you relied on" the fraudulent information. If you knew it was false, you have no claim since you did not rely on it.
5. A Duty of Fair Representation (DFR) lawsuit is almost impossible to win because union attorneys work for the union and not for you. If they feign an effort, the court view the attorney's weakness as your mistake for

employing incompetent attorneys or voting in incompetent representatives. However, if you can prove the "grievance show" is an act, you might have a chance. One pilot did just that, and the union settled because she survived their motion to dismiss phase. The only person I know who won a DFR had a recording of a representative stating "we are not going to represent you." During my grievance, Delta's attorney told the arbitrator that Delta and ALPA were on the same side. The ALPA attorney did not object. I filed a DFR, but the judge did not view that statement was sending a message to the arbitrator. I disagree, but I lost.

6. Arbitrators are businessmen for hire. If your career is on the line, and you have any chance of using federal court in addition to the grievance process—do it!

7. If any chief pilot, management pilot, or employee speaks false and defaming words against you and those statements cause harm, you could file a slander-based defamation of character suit, or libel action if they put it in writing. If you don't have damages, there is no case. You could win but you lose.

8. If any false statements cost you your job or promotion, and you have proof, then go after the person who spoke the damning words. When chief pilots realize they will be held accountable, they may stop doing the company's bidding. Currently the AIR21 statute only allows naming the company, not individuals. But if you have a case of harm caused by an employee you have rights in other courts. Moreover, many State discrimination statutes provide for the personal liability of a supervisor or manager.

9. If the company sends you to neuropsychological testing, you can train. I have placed training documents for such training on my website. They may not be up to date but use Google. That's how I found them, but after I took the tests.[53] I highly recommend you look at them before you go.

10. Settle if you can, but do not give up your job as part of the negotiations unless you do the math and account for taxes to obtain a settlement that is just.

Chapter 16

Unexpected Surprises in the form of Taxes

"The only thing that hurts more than paying an income tax
is not having to pay an income tax."
—*Thomas Dewar*

THE TAX CODE is long, this chapter is short. If you are not currently paying the highest tax bracket, and your company intends on paying your backpay, do not take that in a lump sum. Ensure that the language in the settlement contract identifies the amount received for each year. That way it is *not in a lump sum,* and your accountant can do his magic and refile the taxes for the previous years to include the back pay.

I recommend you discuss the tax situation with your accountant and figure out the best payment plan, so you do not lose anything with a bulk payment. The one person I know who won the DFR took his payments over multiple years to avoid the tax hit on a lump sum.

With hope for a better system, we can find improvement in the law. In the meantime, it's imperative that you take care of yourself in the process. This is the one area that nobody tells you what to expect. Be aware.

Chapter 17

Resilience

"Resilience is all about being able to overcome the unexpected.
Sustainability is about survival.
The goal of resilience is to thrive."
—Jamais Cascio

Survival

IN YOUR DECISION to go to battle, you must be prepared for war. In some cases, the legal system is far more stressful than the action itself, but the option of doing nothing is far worse. I'm not sure if you walk away, that you would not face far worse emotional damage than fighting a good fight and losing. If you did your best, then you should feel proud on that front.

Learn How to Argue

TYPICALLY, I WOULD read motions or briefs and responses that Lee had written, but one day he sent me a Delta filing and told me to take the first crack at it. We had only 30 pages to respond. I had written fifty pages before I was even halfway through their document. I argued each false statement Delta presented. I was so angry that they could write such lies, and I wanted to argue each point. And I did. Damn them all!

This is when Lee told me to not argue false statements, but simply write the truth with supporting facts. The other side will bait you, and you will feel the need to defend each lie. Don't do it. Ignore the false statements and write the facts for the judge to make the decision.

You cannot win an argument with a terrorist or a two-year-old, so don't try. If you write facts and support those facts, that is what the judge will read. The judge won't get involved in the tit for tat argument. And the very reason the bad guys use this tactic to distract you. They throw shit against the wall to see what sticks. It stinks, it doesn't belong there, and you feel the need to wash it off. Don't waste your time.

However, writing the arguments and defense was pure therapy for me, and none of what I wrote remained on the page. I argued my points, and then Lee wrote a cogent response in a manner to win the case. But this experience taught me a great lesson—don't let false assertions get under your skin. They mean nothing. If you need to argue them on paper and save it in a book to get it out, go for it. But if you can take these words of wisdom and go burn their document, releasing the false statements to the wind, do that.

Stick to the facts and do not argue false statements.

Perspective

"My life is not over"

AT THE END of the day, you may be right and still lose. Despite your belief you will succeed, you may not. While I never believed I would lose and always fought for justice, I prepared myself mentally just in case. I knew after doing all I could, the results were not in my hands. Believing you will win is essential, but mentally preparing for if you don't is a good strategy so you are not blindsided.

When I met with a Mayo Clinic psychiatrist, he asked how I was sitting in front of him with such composure after all I had been through. He told me that most people would have been a wreck for all that had happened to date. I told him I was working on a novel titled *Flight for Truth*. He asked if I was in that novel. I explained that I was multiple characters in all my novels, and they all revolved around this event in my life. Fact but with fictional characters and a little murder and sex involved. Then I shared a scene in that book.

Darby and Linda were having a glass of wine discussing Darby's pending visit to the Mayo Clinic the next day, as she, too, faced the challenges I did. Linda, Darby's friend, who happened to be a counselor, told her, *"They may very well get away with this, but your life will not be over, it will just be different."*

I told the doctor that I had to convince myself of this very thing. He smiled and said, "Keep writing," and I did. You, too, must convince yourself that your life won't be over, you may just find another path to follow. File a different flight plan for your life. It might be scary, challenging and not very lucrative at first, but you did it once, you can do it again. This time, with more experience. You will be fine.

Journaling

JOURNALING IS ONE of the best methods to deal with post-traumatic stress disorder (PTSD). My writing novels with actual events simply took journaling to the next level. However, I recently learned that writing third person when you journal is far more powerful by disassociating yourself with the individuals who harmed you by releasing the victim status. Little did I know at the time, but novel writing works.

Ironically, my first novel, *Flight for Control*, was exactly what they accused me of as I had created a sociopathic pilot who intentionally caused pilots to crash their planes. This was prior to Germanwings, and everyone said my book came true when that Germanwings pilot crashed his plane.

The novels, *Flight for Safety, Flight for Survival, Flight for Sanity, Flight for Truth, Flight for Discovery, and Flight for Justice* are all based upon actual events of my experience and this legal case, with more truth than not. Granted I have fictional characters living real life events, but the process of writing may have saved my sanity.

If you read these novels, you'll understand how this writing became therapy, and at the same time addressing the issues in my safety report that have gone unheeded by Delta and the FAA. I took the liberty of adding murder and sinister plots because nobody would believe these events happened simply because a pilot reported safety and management's egos are bigger than their brains. I encourage you to write *your* story to save your sanity. The process is pure therapy and fun. You can legally kill the bad guys.

Forgiveness and Gratitude

Forgiveness, the other F-word.

I BELIEVE IN the power of forgiving and letting go. This does not mean that you condone the behavior, it's simply a method for you to take your life back. I fought like crazy for my career, and then stepped into a legal battle to create change. I got my career back. I won in court. I walked away. I did not get my life back.

Today I can laugh at the stupidity of Delta executives' testimony. I feel empathy for the doctor and attorneys representing evil who take anti-depressants to manage their internal battles of participating in such behavior. This journey was a part of my life that taught me a great deal in both human nature and the law.

I feel gratitude for the ability to have learned the law, and this experience has enabled me to share that knowledge. I feel the greatest gratitude for having the opportunity to meet Lee Seham and all those in his circle who have restored my faith in the legal system and humanity. The opportunity to meet him and his family, and work with his son Sam, were worth the price of admission.

I've also helped many people because of my experience. Granted, there are some who used me for their personal gain, while others who took advantage of my time without respect or consideration. You, too, might experience friends who take a step back or tell you to walk away and ignore what has happened, but that behavior and those suggestions are typically fear based. Their fear has nothing to do with you.

We cannot control what others do, and we cannot expect them to behave as we do. A wise man, Marty Barnhard, told me something so simple when I was trying to get over the negative action of someone, I had thought to be a friend, but only used me. He said, "She is not you."

I suppose we all have a path to follow. And those who inflict harm may be those you least suspect. Such simple words filled with much truth helped me put betrayal into perspective.

With all this said, airline management who think women are an easy target to gaslight should think again. We clean house when the party is over. I tried to clean house to no avail. The dirt and scum were too thick. Therefore, in the eighth novel the clean-up will be in another fashion.

Flight for Revenge is underway. This will be the first novel that is truly fiction because truth will not satisfy the readers, but full accountability might. Lack of accountability should never be an ending to any story. But all too often with the AIR21 law, that is the case.

While I created fictional characters based upon actual people, at the end of the day it's time to torture, kill, and imprison those fictional characters in the most appropriate way.

I hope you're reading this with a smile, because these statements are in the forgiveness section of healing. Which is a reminder, that you need to laugh to heal your life after any legal challenge. Learn how to have fun again. Laugh. Smile. Kill the bad guys on paper and forgive them real-life. Be proud you stood up to them. The most difficult part of this journey is to learn how to move forward and close the chapter.

I have not closed this chapter yet, as I have much work to do. But soon.

Chapter 18
Action Item

"The people who are crazy enough to think they can change the world are the ones who do."
—*Steve Jobs*

Support Needed

THE AIR21 STATUTE protects airline and manufacturer employees from retaliation when they report safety concerns to their employers or the FAA. The law was enacted to improve safety. But the law does not necessarily achieve that goal.

My seven-year intimate experience with the process has made it perfectly clear that airlines and lobbyists ensure that the AIR21 law remains a toothless tiger. Yet, armed with the knowledge in this book you can prevail. Nothing in life is perfect, but always one step forward in effort to make it that way.

At the time of this publication, I had been working to change the AIR21 law for over eight years. Not until the Boeing whistleblower, John Barnett, allegedly killed himself, did others believe that perhaps reform was necessary and jumped in to help.

Authorities found John Barnett in his car holding a gun in his lap with a finger on the trigger. However, that gun had a huge kickback and therefore it might have been an impossible scenario if he had fired it himself. Notwithstanding that there was no blood splatter inside the car, no photographs of the scene were taken, and he had just provided evidence supporting a finding of criminal intent on the part of Boeing. Mr. Barnett had only four hours of deposition remaining the following day.

Having walked in his shoes, I can assert that nobody walks off the field in the fourth quarter of the Super Bowl when they are winning, despite the stress and battering of the game. This leads me to believe that this may have been more than a suicide. But if it were suicide, then the law did not protect him, and post-traumatic stress caused the end of his life.

Post Traumatic Stress Disorder (PTSD) is a killer. While retaliation comes in many forms, and the symptoms of PTSD are many, you do not have to go this journey alone. Beyond the legal battle, there is support available. My friend, Jackie Garrick, has dedicated her life to helping others who face retaliation. As a whistleblower herself, who faced retaliation, she understands the physical and emotional trauma involved, and formed Whistleblowers of America. You are not alone. You are not crazy. There are people who will help you through this challenging time. Reach out to Jackie at: www.whistleblowersofamerica.com.

We cannot bring Mr. Barnett back to life, but at the very least his death will not be in vain. His death ignited others to see the necessity to change the AIR21 law. Actively involved in fighting for the change, below are the final suggestions submitted to congress for AIR21 reform. We need your help to ensure it is passed and becomes reality. Read and sign the petition and help to create change.[54]

GOVERNMENT
ACCOUNTABILITY
PROJECT

MEMORANDUM

FROM: Stakeholders favoring stronger protection for aviation safety advocates.

TO: Relevant Congressional offices and committees

RE: Language to modernize AIR21 protections

The recent death of Boeing whistleblower John Barnett highlights the inadequacy of protections under the AIR21 statute. 49 U.S.C. §42121(a). The Boeing fiascos are *déjà vu* about a quality control breakdown that could and should have been corrected long ago. Mr. Barnett had been protesting for over a decade, initially through the Boeing corporation and then through current legal rights (the AIR21 procedural mechanisms) that proceeded at a molasses pace. When anti-retaliation rights in AIR21 were first enacted in 2000, they reflected best practices at the time. Over a decade later, however, they have become badly outdated and now are primitive compared to 16 corporate whistleblower laws that Congress subsequently enacted unanimously. While some additional amendments have been made to AIR21 in recent years, Barnett's death and the ongoing significant safety failures with airplanes demonstrate that AIR21 must be strengthened to encourage workers in the industry to speak up before passengers are harmed. The suggestions below are for an AIR21 Safety Advocate Act, which we think the current law should be renamed.

AIR21: Delta's Debacle

These recommendations are the menu of where AIR21 needs updating to keep pace with other corporate accountability laws, and include language to provide solutions.

1. **Lack of anti-gag shield**. Corporations routinely try to suppress employee speech, ranging from a condition of employment to gag orders concealing specific misconduct. Also, many employees must waive their statutory due process remedies. Vulnerability to these restrictions can render AIR21 rights meaningless. Every corporate whistleblower law since AIR21, as well as the civil service Whistleblower Protection Act, have boilerplate supremacy of law "anti-gag" provisions to cancel out any job prerequisites that would override statutory rights.

Proposed solution: Add a new §42121(e): NONENFORCE-ABILITY OF CERTAIN PROVISIONS WAIVING RIGHTS AND REMEDIES OR REQUIRING ARBITRATION OF DISPUTES.—

  (1) WAIVER OF RIGHTS AND REMEDIES. —The rights and remedies provided for in this section may not be waived by any agreement, policy, form, or condition of employment, including by a pre-dispute arbitration agreement.

  (2) PREDISPUTE ARBITRATION AGREEMENTS. — No pre-dispute arbitration agreement shall be valid or enforceable, to the extent the agreement requires arbitration of a dispute arising under this section.

2. **Statute of limitations**. The current 90-day statute of limitations to file a retaliation claim is an unrealistic, statutory relic. For many forms of retaliation (i.e. cancelation of medical or retirement benefits, vacations, or retaliatory investigations/dossiers) victims may not even know it occurred for the first three months. Moreover, employers may string the whistleblower along with its own appeal procedures that go beyond the 90-day period. The current best practice is three years from when the whistleblower learns of retaliation, but a minimum of 180 days can be found in other laws.

Proposed solution: Modify 49 U.S.C. §42121(b)(1) as follows: FILING AND NOTIFICATION -- A person who believes that he or she has been discharged or otherwise discriminated against by any person in violation of subsection (a) may, not later than *three years* **after** *learning of* such violation, file (or have any person file on his or her behalf) a complaint with the Secretary of Labor alleging such discharge or discrimination. In addition, where the employer offers an employee an appeal or grievance process, the time period accrues upon the final decision of such process.

3. Absence of "kickout" for due process. Mr. Barnett filed his AIR21 complaint with the Department of Labor in January 2017 and it took almost four years for the Occupational Safety and Health Administration (OSHA) to complete its investigation. Mr. Barnett appealed the denial of his claim to the Office of Administrative Law Judges, where Boeing was able to delay the proceeding by employing dilatory discovery tactics that resulted in the judge ordering Boeing twice to produce records. Mr. Barnett was first deposed more than seven years after filing his complaint. Justice delayed is justice denied. It is not uncommon for OSHA to take three or more years to issue a non-enforceable initial determination, and in FY 2023 OSHA ruled against the whistleblowers in nearly all cases.

With these routine delays, the whistleblower's disclosures have faded into historical background. Informal or solely administrative adjudication is inadequate to serve as the sole channel for whistleblowers to pursue their claims. That is why all 16 corporate whistleblower laws enacted since AIR21 include a "kick-out" safety valve option: if DOL does not issue a final decision within 180 or 210 days, the whistleblower can move the case to federal court with a clean slate for a jury trial. For credible rights, air safety whistleblowers must have the option to remove their claims for a due process hearing, in federal court including if administrative proceedings are not timely. Additionally, whistleblower litigators we consulted with have noted that because of the power imbalance that exists (with airlines' high powered and seemingly endless budget), it is important for whistleblowers to make the decision whether the case would be heard by an administrative law judge or jury.

<u>Proposed solution</u>: Renumber § 42121(b)(2)(B) to (C) and add a new subparagraph (B) as follows: *If the Secretary has not issued a final decision within sixty (60) days of the filing of the complaint, the complainant may proceed with a de novo hearing before an Administrative Law Judge of the Office of Administrative Law Judges of the United States Department of Labor.*

Add a new § 42121(b)(7) as follows:

If the Secretary has not issued a final decision within 180 days of the filing of the complaint and there is no showing that such delay is due to the bad faith of the claimant, the plaintiff may bring an action at law or equity for de novo review in the appropriate district court of the United States, which shall have jurisdiction with a jury trial at the plaintiff's request over such an action without regard to the amount in controversy.

4. Coverage gaps. The current law still doesn't cover all those who may have evidence vital to prevent or properly investigate air safety tragedies. Despite an important update several years ago, we continue to believe that more can be done in this regard. The law should protect all whose activities are governed by Title 49. To defend against blacklisting, applicants and former employees must be protected. Further, like the False Claims Act and Dodd Frank, citizens such as air crash victims and families should have the right to bear witness safely.

Proposed solution: Modify 49 U.S.C. §42121(a) as follows: "Prohibited Discrimination.-*Any employer whose activities are governed by and engaging in activities subject to this Title,* holder of a certificate under section 44704 or 44705 of this title, or a contractor, subcontractor, or supplier of such holder, *or any officer, employee, contractor, subcontractor, or agent of the employer may not discriminate against any person, including an applicant,* employee *or former employee* may not discharge an employee or otherwise discriminate against an employee with respect to compensation, terms, conditions, or privileges of employment because the employee *or person* (or any person acting pursuant to a request of *or associated with* the employee *or person*) including as part of the job duties of the individual or individuals."

5. Deterrence through personal liability and damages

Because AIR21 defendants can only be corporations, not individuals who retaliated, the law has no deterrent impact on corporate "hatchet men" who carry out retaliation. The worst that can happen is they won't get away with it, and history shows they almost certainly will be rewarded with promotions or bonuses for doing the dirty work of harassment. The landmark Sarbanes-Oxley law cured this defect by permitting suits to include the individuals who carry out harassment to be defendants. That principle of personal accountability should be extended to AIR21. For the same reason, some corporate whistleblower laws provide punitive damages. Due to the high public policy stakes, these teeth for deterrence should be added to AIR21.

Proposed solution: (incorporated in prior recommendation as well) Amend §42121(a) as follows: "A holder of a certificate under section 44704 or 44705 of this title, or *an employee, officer*, contractor, subcontractor, supplier *or agent* of such holder, may not discharge an employee or otherwise discriminate…

6. Absence of protection for refusing to violate the law. Sometimes making noise is not enough to prevent a tragedy. It is necessary to walk the talk by refusing to violate the law. The federal Whistleblower Protection Act and an increasing number of corporate whistleblower laws have recognized this basic truth and provided anti-retaliation rights for refusing to violate the law. In light of the life and death stakes for air safety violations, whistleblowers should be able safely to opt out of illegality that puts the public at risk.

Proposed solution: Add a new §42121(a)(5) as follows: *"objected to, or refused to participate in, any activity, policy, practice, or assigned task that the employee (or other such person) reasonably believed to be in violation of any law, rule, order, standard, or prohibition, subject to the jurisdiction of, or enforceable by, the Administration."*

7. Absence of temporary relief. As discussed above, it is not unusual for cases to take over five years for a final decision. That often means it is too late for the victory to neutralize retaliation. The whistleblower already has often gone bankrupt, lost all credibility in the profession, and often lost their home and family. We liken it to a doctor who provides a heart transplant after the patient has died. Employers know this and drag out proceedings shamelessly. For rights to be functional, if the employee meets their burden to prove a *prima facie* case, it is necessary to provide temporary relief while the case proceeds. This also will reduce unnecessary litigation delays and promote settlement, as employers no longer will have an incentive to delay proceedings in which they are winning for practical consequences until a final decision.

Proposed solution: Add a new §42121(b)(8) as follows: ***"At any time after filing an action, a complainant may seek a stay to provide temporary relief while the action is ongoing to enjoin any alleged discrimination. The Secretary or federal court with jurisdiction shall order a stay if after a hearing the plaintiff has satisfied their burden to present a prima facie case under §42121(b)(2)(B) by demonstrating that protected activity was a contributing factor to the alleged discrimination. The motion for a stay shall be heard no later than 90 days after such motion is filed. In the event a complainant prevails before the Administrative Law Judge, the ALJ would proceed with the assessment and award of interim attorney's fees, which will be payable irrespective of the pendency of an appeal to the Administrative Review Board or court."***

8. **Mandatory posting of rights**. All too often, neither employees nor managers are aware of AIR21's anti-retaliation rights. This was the case involving Boeing South Carolina, where numerous whistleblowers were unaware of AIR21. Having missed the 90-day statute of limitations deadline, they filed in Federal District Court, where their cases were dismissed because AIR21 was their exclusive remedy. Corporate whistleblower laws routinely have a requirement missing from AIR21 – mandatory posting of rights in the law. A trend in global whistleblower laws is requiring employers to provide training for employees and managers in the rights. The knowledge loophole in AIR21 should be closed with mandatory posting and training. These measures are necessary for rights on paper to take root in reality.

<u>Suggested solution</u>: Add a new §42121(b)(9) as follows: Any employer subject to this Act shall provide prominent physical and internet posting, and provide initial and annual training, to all employees on the rights and remedies available under this Act.

9. Rights that are additive, not substitutive for existing remedies. In addition to AIR21, aviation whistleblowers can currently try to defend themselves through other remedies. They may make other claims under state laws, such as public polity exception tort suits, defamation, physical injury or other torts, and breach of contract. Employers frequently argue that whistleblower statutes cancel out all alternative claims. While those attacks run counter to majority precedents, to be safe AIR21 like other corporate laws should add a noncontroversial clarifying amendment as exists in other Labor Department whistleblower statutes that it is not a substitute for other remedies.

<u>Proposed solution</u>: Add a new clarifying amendment to §42121(b)(10) as follows: ***"RIGHTS RETAINED.—Nothing in this section shall be deemed to diminish the rights, privileges, or remedies of any whistleblower under any Federal or State law or under any collective bargaining agreement."***

Further, amend 42121(b)(3) as follows: ***"(iii) provide compensatory and punitive damages to the complainant."***

<u>10. Agency investigations of whistleblowing disclosures</u>. The whole point of risking retaliation is to expose and correct air safety violations, but AIR21 is limited to defending against retaliation. Department of Labor regulations call for referral of disclosures for agency investigation of alleged misconduct, but the FAA routinely fails to follow through. Analogous to surface transportation statutes that refer disclosures for agency investigations, AIR21 should require the FAA to investigate the evidence of alleged misconduct whenever there is a finding the whistleblower demonstrates a *prima facie* case of retaliation. Equivalent to the Whistleblower Protection Act for federal employees, the whistleblower should have an opportunity to provide comments included in the final report.

Proposed solution: Add a new §42121(b)(8) as follows: *"Whenever a representative of the Secretary of Labor makes a determination in proceedings before the Department that the complainant has satisfied their burden to present a prima facie case under §42121(b)(2)(B), the Secretary shall communicate that finding and associated evidence to the Administrator, who shall conduct an examination of the complainant's disclosure and provide the complainant the opportunity to provide comments included in the report of investigation. The Complainant will be provided the final report in compliance with privacy law requirements."*

11. Enforcement of OSHA Orders of Reinstatement: Several court decisions have held that a preliminary order of reinstatement issued by OSHA upon the conclusion of an investigation is not enforceable because Congress did not confer federal judicial power to enforce preliminary orders of reinstatement. *See, e.g., Bechtel v. Competitive Techs., Inc.,* 448 F.3d 469, 473 (2d Cir. 2006); *Gulden v. Exxon Mobil Corp.*, No. 3:22-cv-7418, 2023 WL 3004854 (D.N.J. Apr. 19, 2023); *Solis v. Union Pac. R.R. Co.*, No. 12-394, 2013 WL 440707 (D. Idaho Jan. 11, 2013).

Proposed solution: Amend § 42121(b)(2)(A) as follows: (2) INVESTIGATION: PRELIMINARY ORDER (A) In general.-Not later than 60 days after the date of receipt of a complaint filed under paragraph (1) and after affording the person named in the complaint an opportunity to submit to the Secretary of Labor a written response to the complaint and an opportunity to meet with a representative of the Secretary to present statements from witnesses, the Secretary of Labor shall conduct an investigation and determine whether there is reasonable cause to believe that the complaint has merit and notify, in writing, the complainant and the person alleged to have committed a violation of subsection (a) of the Secretary's findings. If the Secretary of Labor concludes that there is a reasonable cause to believe that a violation of subsection (a) has occurred, the Secretary shall accompany the Secretary's findings with a preliminary order providing the relief prescribed by paragraph (3)(B). Not later than 30 days after the date of notification of findings under this paragraph, either the person alleged to have committed the violation or the complainant may file objections to the findings or preliminary order, or both, and request a hearing on the record. The filing of such objections shall not operate to stay any reinstatement remedy contained in the preliminary order. Such hearings shall be conducted expeditiously. If a hearing is not requested in such 30-day period, the preliminary order shall be deemed a final order that is not subject to judicial review. *Whenever any person has failed to comply with a preliminary order of reinstatement issued under this paragraph, the Secretary of Labor or the complainant may file a civil action in the United States district court for the district in which the violation was found to occur to enforce such order. In actions brought under this paragraph, the district courts shall have jurisdiction to grant all appropriate relief including, but not limited to, injunctive relief.*

12. **Extraterritorial application of AIR21:** The ARB has held that Congress did not expressly authorize extraterritorial application of AIR21, and therefore the statute applies only to violations that occur within U.S. borders. *See, e.g., Shi v. Moog, Inc.*, ARB No. 2017-0072, ALJ No. 2016-AIR-00020 (ARB Dec. 5, 2019). But as discussed in an opinion by a former Chief Department of Labor Administrative Law Judge, the purpose of AIR21 warrants extraterritorial application of the statute:

Just as the predominant purpose of Section 806 of SOX is fraud detection, the predominant purpose of Section 42121 is detection of aviation safety hazards and airline non-compliance with FAA safety laws, rules and regulations . . . AIR21 provides an incentive to airline workers which promotes aviation safety inasmuch as "it provides job security . . . as a means of encouraging employees voluntarily to take an action Congress deems in the public interest." Id. at 13. . . . AIR21's legislative history also indicates that AIR21's whistleblower protection provision is just one of many aviation safety mechanisms in a statute that holds aviation safety as its preeminent goal. For example, each time AIR21's whistleblower provision was specifically mentioned during the congressional floor debates preceding the statute's enactment, it was discussed as a mechanism for further ensuring aviation safety, and at no point did a legislator suggest that Section 42121's purpose is to regulate labor conditions in the industry. See, e.g., 146 Cong. Rec. S1247-07, S1252 (daily ed. March 8, 2000) (statement of Sen. Grassley) ("whistle-blower protection adds another, much needed, layer of protection for the traveling public using our Nation's air transportation system."); 146 Cong. Rec. S1255-01 at S1257 (statement of Sen. Hollings) (AIR21 includes "whistleblower protection to aid in our safety efforts and protect workers willing to expose safety problems."); 146 Cong. Rec. H1002-01 at H1008 (statement of Rep. Boehlert) (AIR21 "provide[s]whistle-blower protection for both FAA and airline employees so they can reveal legitimate safety problems without fear of retaliation.").

Dos Santos v. Delta Airlines, Inc., 2012-AIR-20 (ALJ Jan. 11, 2013) Absent express clarification that the statute applies extraterritorially, whistleblowers will not be protected if a violation occurs abroad, despite it being a U.S. carrier subject to U.S. law.

Proposed solution: Add a new §42121(f) as follows: "EXTRA-TERRITORIAL JURISDICTION. The rights and remedies provided for in this section shall apply extraterritorially, including but not limited to any violation committed by a covered employer operating outside United States territory.

13. Constructive resolution: Whether retaliation cases are resolved at the administrative level or in court, as a rule litigation inherently means an ugly-prolonged, draining process for both parties. A constructive resolution is far preferable. When the Wage and Hour Division administered the first phase of reprisal complaints, its first effort consistently was acting as a mediator seeking to prevent unnecessary conflict. Since OSHA replaced Wage and Hour, however, DOL efforts to settle complaints have become the exception rather than the rule. Recent agency investigation manual provisions have revived Alternative Disputes Resolution as an option during initial investigations. That development should be institutionalized as a mandatory responsibility.

Proposed solution: Amend 42121(b)(2) as follows: (2) INVESTIGATION: PRELIMINARY ORDER

A) In general.-Not later than 60 days after the date of receipt of a complaint filed under paragraph (1) and after affording the person named in the complaint an opportunity to submit to the Secretary of Labor a written response to the complaint and an opportunity to meet with a representative of the Secretary to present statements from witnesses, the Secretary of Labor shall conduct an investigation and determine whether there is reasonable cause to believe that the complaint has merit and notify, in writing, the complainant and the person alleged to have committed a violation of subsection (a) of the Secretary's findings. *If either party requests, the Secretary shall attempt to resolve the complaint through an Alternative Disputes Mechanism procedure agreed to by both parties.* If the Secretary of Labor concludes that there is a reasonable cause to believe that a violation of subsection (a) has occurred, the Secretary shall accompany the Secretary's findings with a preliminary order providing the relief prescribed by paragraph (3)(B). Not later than 30 days after the date of notification of findings under this paragraph, either the person alleged to have committed the violation or the complainant may file objections to the findings or preliminary order, or both, and request a hearing on the record. The filing of such objections shall not operate to stay any reinstatement remedy contained in the preliminary order. Such hearings shall be conducted expeditiously. If a hearing is not requested in such 30-day period, the preliminary order shall be deemed a final order that is not subject to judicial review.

14. **Attorney fees:** A common litigation tactic is to act noncooperatively during pre-hearing or trial discovery, refusing to provide documents or witnesses voluntarily until a specific ruling by the judge. This obstructive tactic prolongs the disputes and significantly increases costs for the whistleblower. Unfortunately, some precedents have denied attorney fee reimbursements for these costs. The impact is that whistleblowers can still lose by winning, because they are saddled with uncompensated expenses. All costs incurred, whether before OSHA at the preliminary stage or during due process discovery disputes, must be compensated for the whistleblower to be made whole.

Proposed solution: Amend 49121(b)(3)(B) as follows:

(B) REMEDY - If, in response to a complaint filed under paragraph (1), the Secretary of Labor determines that a violation of subsection (a) has occurred, the Secretary of Labor shall order, the person who committed such violation to

(i) take affirmative action to abate the violation;

> (ii) reinstate the complainant to his or her former position together with the compensation (including back pay) and restore the terms, conditions, and privileges associated with his or her employment; and
> (iii) provide compensatory and punitive damages to the complainant.
>
> If such an order is issued under this paragraph, the Secretary of Labor, at the request of the complainant, shall assess against the person against whom the order is issued a sum equal to the aggregate amount of all costs and expenses (including attorneys' and expert witness fees reasonably incurred, as determined by the Secretary of Labor, by the complainant for, or in connection with, the bringing the complaint upon which the order was issued *and necessary to prevail in the action.*

Contact information: For further information, any questions or concerns, please contact **Maya Efrati with the Government Accountability Project** (<mefrati@whistleblower.org>).

References

Introduction
1. *Petitt vs. Delta*: 2018-AIR-00041

Chapter 1
2. Wendell H. Ford Aviation Investment and Reform Act for the 21st Century (AIR21) 49 U.S.C. §42121: https://www.whistleblowers.gov/statutes/air21
3. OSHA Fact Sheet Appendix A
4. OSHA Fact Sheet Appendix A
5. Seham, Seham Meltz and Peterson: https://www.ssmplaw.com/attorneys/sehamlee/Lee's Link to LIRR Safety
6. OSHA Fact Sheet Appendix A
7. How to File an AIR21 Whistleblower Complaint, How to Notify the Department of Labor/OSHA https://www.faa.gov/about/initiatives/whistleblower/complaint

Chapter 2
8. OSHA Fact Sheet Appendix A
9. KNKT.18.10.35.04 (2019) *Aircraft Accident Investigation Report PT. Lion Mentari Airlines Boeing 737-8 (MAX)*; PK-LQP Tanjung Karawang, West Java Republic of Indonesia, 29 October 2018
10. NTSB (2023) *Response to Final Aircraft Accident Investigation Report Ethiopian Airlines Flight 302 Boeing 737-8 MAX, ET-AVJ Ejere, Ethiopia March 10, 2019*
11. DOT (2023) *Implementation and Oversight of the Aircraft Certification, Safety, and Accountability.* https://www.

transportation.gov/implementation-and-oversight-
aircraft-certification-safety-and-accountability-act

12. https://linknky.com/business/2021/12/23/boone-county-
jury-awards-nearly-2/

13. https://whistleblower.house.gov/office-whistleblower-
ombuds

Chapter 4

14. Petitt, Karlene Kassner, *"Safety Culture, Training,
Understanding, Aviation Passion: The Impact on Manual
Flight and Operational Performance"* (2019). Doctoral
Dissertations and Master's Theses. 436. https://commons.
erau.edu/edt/436

15. OSHA Fact Sheet Appendix A

Chapter 5

16. Perrow, C. (1999). *Normal accidents. Living with high-risk
technologies.* West Sussex, UK: Princeton University Press.

17. Helmreich, R. L., Merritt, A. C., & Wilhelm, J. A. (1999).
*The evolution of crew resource management training in
commercial aviation.* The International Journal of Aviation
Psychology, 9(1), 19–32. doi:10.1207/s15327108ijap0901_2
PMID:11541445

18. Doc. No. FAA-2009-0023, 76 FR 3837, Jan. 21, 2011. 14
CFR § 135.330 - *Crew resource management training.*

19. Nemeth, L., (2015, November 4). *Using safety data to
improve training and ultimately safety.* In 68th Annual
International Air Safety Summit, Miami, FL.

20. 14 CFR § 121.909 - Approval of Advanced Qualification
Program.

21. Helmreich, R.L. & Klinect, J.R. & Wilhelm, J.A.. (2001).
System safety and threat and error management: The
line operations safety audit (LOSA). Proceedings of
the Eleventh International Symposium on Aviation,
Psychology. 1-6.

22. FAA (2023) Final report: *Safety Culture: A Significant
Influence on Safety in Transportation*

Chapter 6

23. Estbrook v. Federal Express (2017) *Decision and Order denying relief.* 2014-AIR-00022
24. FAA (2024) *Safety Management Systems* **14 CFR** Chapter 1 subchapter A part 5 https://www.ecfr.gov/current/title-14/chapter-I/subchapter-A/part-5
25. YouTube (2019) *Delta CEO Ed Bastian 1: I dont' know what accountable executive means* https://www.youtube.com/watch?v=pa5wer0KKY4&t=1673s
26. Bastian Dep. 37:19- 38:6, Feb. 27, 2019.
27. Petitt v. Delta, Volume I, Robert Ohlson, Direct Testimony p 155, (March 25, 2019)

Chapter 7

28. FAA (2024) *Aviation Safety Action Program (ASAP)* https://www.faa.gov/about/initiatives/asap
29. Sumwalt, R. (2022) *Convinced That you Have A Good Safety Culture?* Aviation Week Network. https://aviationweek.com/business-aviation/safety-ops-regulation/convinced-you-have-good-safety-culture
30. FAA (2024) *Aviation Safety Action Program (ASAP)* https://www.faa.gov/about/initiatives/asap
31. FAA (2024) *Safety Management System (SMS)* https://www.faa.gov/about/initiatives/sms

Chapter 8

32. Petitt v. Delta, Volume I, Robert Ohlson, Direct Testimony p 52, (March 25, 2019).

Chapter 9

33. OSHA Fact Sheet Appendix A
34. Lownsbury v Van Buren, 762 NE2d 354 (Ohio 2002). State v Herendeen et al, 279 Ga 323, 613 SE2d 647 (Ga 2005).
35. Captain Martin "Marty" Barnard Email: marty.barnard@yahoo.com
36. Captain Mike Danford Email: n0kkj@yahoo.com

37. Petitt, Karlene (2024), "PEth Testing False Positives", Mendeley Data, V1, doi: 10.17632/fg3r3gf7rj.1

Chapter 10
38. Petitt v. Delta, Volume I, Robert Ohlson, Opening Statement p 21, (March 25, 2019)
39. *Clark v. Pace Airlines, Inc., ARB No. 04-150, ALJ No. 2003-AIR-28 (ARB Nov. 30, 2006), slip op. at 12-13,*

Chapter 11
40. FAA (2022) *How to File an AIR21 Whistleblower Complaint* https://www.faa.gov/about/initiatives/whistleblower/complaint
41. US DOL (2024) *Occupational Safety and Health Administration: Whistleblower Protection Program* https://www.whistleblowers.gov/

Chapter 13
42. Petitt v. Delta, Decision and Order Granting Relief, 2018-AIR-00041
43. Gates, D. (2022) *Delta 'weaponized' mental health rules against a pilot. She fought back,* Seattle Times Boeing and Aerospace. https://www.seattletimes.com/business/boeing-aerospace/delta-weaponized-mental-health-rules-against-a-pilot-she-fought-back/
44. YouTube (2019) *Delta CEO Ed Bastian 1: I dont' know what accountable executive means* https://www.youtube.com/watch?v=pa5wer0KKY4&t=1673s

Chapter 14
45. Petitt v. Delta, Decision and Order Granting Relief, 2018-AIR-00041
46. KarlenePetitt.com Advocacy Tab: Timeline
47. Petitt v. Delta, Volume IX, Robert Ohlson, Direct Testimony p 143, (May 1, 2019).
48. Petitt v. Delta, Volume, V, Robert Ohlson, Direct Testimony

p 135, (March 29, 2019).

49. FOIA.Gov *How Do I Make a FOIA Request* https://www.foia.gov/how-to.html

50. KarlenePetitt.com Advocacy tab: ESI

51. Kathryn A (2023) *ChatGPT: US lawyer admits using AI for case research.* BBC https://www.bbc.com/news/world-us-canada-65735769

52. Petitt v. Delta, Volume IX, Robert Ohlson, Direct Testimony p 151, (May 1, 2019).

53. KarlenePetitt.com Advocacy tab: Mental Health Training

Chapter 17

54. Website: KarlenePetitt.com ADVOCACY: Sign the Petition

APPENDIX A

OSHA *FactSheet*

Whistleblower Protection for Employees in the Aviation Industry

CERTAIN AVIATION INDUSTRY employers are prohibited from retaliating against employees for reporting alleged violations of federal laws related to aviation safety or engaging in other protected activities.

The Wendell H. Ford Aviation Investment and Reform Act for the 21st Century (AIR21), 49 U.S.C. § 42121, provides retaliation protections for employees of air carriers, certain aircraft manufacturers and designers, and employees of their contractors, subcontractors, or suppliers.

Covered Employees

Under AIR21, employees of the following types of employers are protected from retaliation for engaging in certain protected activities related to aviation safety:

Air carriers (holders of an air carrier operating certificate under 49 U.S.C. § 44705)

Aircraft manufacturers and designers (holders of type, supplemental type, production, or airworthiness certificates under 49 U.S.C. § 44704)

Such entities' contractors performing functions related to aviation safety, subcontractors, and suppliers

Protected Activity

If your employer is covered under AIR21, it may not discharge or in any other manner retaliate against you because you provided information to, are about to provide information to, or caused information to be provided to your employer or the Federal government relating to any violation or alleged violation of any order, regulation, or standard of the Federal Aviation Administration (FAA) or any other provision of Federal law relating aviation safety.

Your employer may not discharge or in any manner retaliate against you because you filed, caused to be filed, testified in, participated in, or assisted in a proceeding under one of these categories of law.

Also, your employer may not discharge or in any other manner retaliate against you for refusing to perform work assignments that you reasonably believe would cause you to violate any order, regulation, or standard of the FAA or any other provision of Federal law relating to aviation safety.

What Is Retaliation?

Retaliation is an adverse action against an employee because of activity protected by AIR21. Retaliation can include several types of actions, such as:

- Firing or laying off
- Demoting
- Denying overtime or promotion
- Disciplining
- Denying benefits
- Failure to hire or rehire
- Intimidation or harassment
- Making threats
- Reassignment to a less desirable position or actions affecting promotion prospects
- Reducing pay or hours
- More subtle actions, such as isolating, ostracizing, mocking, or falsely accusing the employee of poor performance
- Blacklisting (intentionally interfering with an employee's ability to obtain future employment)
- Constructive discharge (quitting when an employer makes working conditions intolerable due to the employee's protected activity)

- Reporting the employee to the police or immigration authorities

Deadline for Filing Complaints

Complaints must be filed within 90 days after the employee learns of the alleged adverse action.

How to File an AIR21 Complaint

An employee, or an employee's representative, can file an AIR21 complaint with OSHA by visiting or calling the local OSHA office, sending a written complaint to the closest OSHA office, or filing a complaint online. No particular form is required and complaints may be submitted in any language.

Written complaints may be filed by fax, electronic communication, hand delivery during business hours, U.S. mail (confirmation services recommended), or other third-party commercial carrier.

The date of the postmark, fax, electronic communication, telephone call, hand delivery, delivery to a third-party commercial carrier, or in-person filing at an OSHA office is considered the date filed.

To file a complaint electronically, please visit www.osha.gov/whistleblower/WBComplaint.

To contact an OSHA area office, please call 1-800-321-OSHA (6742) to be connected to the closest area office. Or visit our website at www.osha.gov/contactus/bystate and click on your state to find your local OSHA office address and contact information.

When OSHA receives a complaint, the agency will first review it to determine whether certain basic requirements are met, such as whether the complaint was filed on time. If so, the complaint will then be investigated according to the procedures required by 29 CFR Part 1979.

Results of the Investigation

If the evidence supports an employee's complaint of retaliation and a settlement cannot be reached, OSHA will issue an order requiring the employer to, as appropriate, put the employee back to work, pay lost wages, restore benefits, and provide other possible relief. The exact requirements will depend on the facts of the case. If the evidence does not support the employee's complaint, OSHA will dismiss the complaint.

After OSHA issues a decision, the employer and/or the employee may request a full hearing before an administrative law judge of the Department of Labor. The administrative law judge's decision may be appealed to the Department's Administrative Review Board (ARB). The ARB's decision is subject to review by the Secretary of Labor, and a final decision may be appealed to a court of appeals.

To Get Further Information

For a copy of the AIR21 whistleblower provision, 49 U.S.C. § 42121, the regulations (29 CFR Part 1979), and other information, go to www.whistleblowers.gov.

OSHA's Whistleblower Protection Programs enforce the whistleblower provisions of more than twenty federal whistleblower laws. To learn more about the whistleblower statutes that OSHA enforces, view our "Whistleblower Statutes Desk Aid" at www.whistleblowers.gov/whistleblower_acts-desk_reference.pdf.

For information on the Office of Administrative Law Judges procedures and case law research materials, go to www.dol.gov/agencies/oalj/topics/information/Information_for_Whistleblowers.

To obtain more information about Federal laws relating to air carrier safety and FAA regulations and standards, please visit the FAA website at www.faa.gov.

Under the Occupational Safety and Health Act of 1970, employers are responsible for providing safe and healthful workplaces for their employees. OSHA's role is to ensure these conditions for America's workers by setting and enforcing standards, and providing training, education, and assistance. For more information, visit www.osha.gov.

This is one in a series of informational fact sheets highlighting OSHA programs, policies or standards. It does not impose any new compliance requirements. For a comprehensive list of compliance requirements of OSHA standards or regulations, refer to Title 29 of the Code of Federal Regulations. This information will be made available to sensory-impaired individuals upon request. The voice phone is (202) 693-1999; teletypewriter (TTY) number: 1-877-889-5627. DWPP FS-3670 02/2023

APPENDIX B
Legal Terrms

Admissions: Statements acknowledging the truth of fact.

AIR21 Whistleblower Statute: A Law protecting airline, aircraft manufacturers, and contractor employees from retaliation who report protected activity.

ALJ: Administrative Law Judge. Administrative law judges are executive judges for hearings of administrative disputes in the Federal government. They only hear administrative issues designated in the Administrative Procedure Act of 1946 (APA) and are part of the executive branch, not the judicial branch, appointed by the heads of the executive agencies.

AMAS: Aviation Medical Advisory. This group, once called ALPA Medical Advisory Services, supported only ALPA pilots' medical needs but expanded to profit from others in aviation who seek their assistance. ALPA members' dues pay for this service for ALPA pilots.

ARB: Administrative Review Board. Department of labor appeal process for cases arising from worker protection laws, including whistleblower and public contract laws.

Bates Stamping: A method of sequentially numbering legal documents, with a reference number beyond the page number. Such as Dr. Altman page 125 would be Bates stamped DA 125.

Compensatory Damages: Payment to make an employee whole to included out of pocket expenses and lost pay.

Complainant: The person filing the complaint.

Contingency Fee: The payment to a lawyer for their legal services in which fee is established prior to trial, to be paid after a win instead of an hourly rate.

Decision and Order: The ruling

Defendant: The company or person that you filed charges against.

ESI: Notice of Need and Demand to Preserve Electronically stored Information

ICAO: International Civil Aviation Organization.

Interrogatories: A written set of questions from one party in a case by another party of which must be answered.

Interlocutory Review: An appeal for part of the case, of which one of the parties filed for the review to not have to wait for a final verdict to receive necessary and immediate recourse.

Motion to Compel: A formal request of the Court to require a party or a non-party in a lawsuit to comply with a discovery request such as a request for production, request for admission, interrogatory request, or subpoena.

NDA: Non-disclosure agreement. You can't tell anyone what the bad guys did.

Plaintiff: Another word meaning Complainant, which is you.

Pro Se: When you decided to defend yourself without an attorney.

Prima Facie Case: When the pre-trial evidence, reviewed by a judge, is sufficient to justify the trial of which the burden of proof is on you, the Complainant.

Punitive damages: Payments with the intent to punish the perpetrator.

RLA: Railway Labor Act: An Archaic Law formed in 1926 governing railroad workers and then subsequently airline employees. This is where special bargaining dispute resolution procedures apply to the railway and airline. The RLA is administered by the National Mediation Board ("NMB"), an independent Federal agency and, in my opinion should be done away with.

Statute: A written law

War of Attrition: When your company ensures the battle that turns into a several year war of which they can financially sustain the fight and legally drain your resources.

From the Author

WHILE THIS BOOK is based upon actual events of my AIR21 case with lessons learned, there is more to this story. I encapsulated the gist of what transpired in a series of novels. While the first novel was based on Industry issues, those that followed include facts of what Delta did in response to my safety concerns, and their attack with a mental health accusation. The novels journey through Delta safety lapses, the evaluation process, my subsequent filing an AIR21 lawsuit and fighting for the truth, along with the discovery process, and the fight for Justice. This entire process was about the fight for safety, followed by my survival. Granted, there is sex and violence in the novels, with sinister plots, because nobody would believe airline employees and executives alike would do as they did simply for ego, power and money. I changed the names in the novels to protect the guilty and my job, as I was still employed while authoring the fictional version of the truth. Now retired, without an NDA, I can share all. More to come on that. But the truth is scarier than fiction.

- *Flight For Control*
- *Flight For Safety*
- *Flight For Survival*
- *Flight For Sanity*
- *Flight For Truth*
- *Flight For Discovery*
- *Flight For Justice*
- *Flight For Revenge* (coming soon)

Check out my website at KarlenePetitt.com

Gratitude:

To all those who support the truth and are willing to fight for justice, I am grateful. To my husband always. To Lee Seham for ensuring my legal facts were accurate. And to Nathan Everett at Elder Road Books for helping this book come to life!

About the Author

DR. KARLENE PETITT holds a PhD in Aviation, MBA and MHS degrees. After forty years of airline flying, instructing, and writing training programs she finally retired as a Delta captain. She holds nine type ratings—B727, B737, B757, B767, B747-200, B747-400, B777, A330, and A350, and is now working as an aviation safety consultant. She lives with her husband, Dick, and they commute between Palm Desert and Seattle, while they both work on their golf games.

Made in United States
North Haven, CT
15 July 2025

70724305R00098